Doing Ethical Research with Children

Doing Ethical Research with Children

Jonathon Sargeant and Deborah Harcourt

Open University Press

Open University Press
McGraw-Hill Education
McGraw-Hill House
Shoppenhangers Road
Maidenhead
Berkshire
England
SL6 2QL

email: enquiries@openup.co.uk
world wide web: www.openup.co.uk

and Two Penn Plaza, New York, NY 10121-2289, USA

First published 2012

A catalogue record of this book is available from the British Library

ISBN-13: 978-0-33-524642-7 (pb)
ISBN-10: 0-33-524642-7 (pb)   *20 11000 540*
eISBN: 978-0-33-524643-4

Library of Congress Cataloging-in-Publication Data
CIP data applied for

Typesetting and e-book compilations by
RefineCatch Limited, Bungay, Suffolk
Printed in the UK by Bell & Bain Ltd, Glasgow

Fictitious names of companies, products, people, characters and/or data that may be
used herein (in case studies or in examples) are not intended to represent any real
individual, company, product or event.

The **McGraw-Hill** Companies

"Doing Ethical Research with Children *provides an invaluable guide to understanding and managing the ethical implications of research projects with children. The highly accessible format includes useful case-study examples, questions and checklists and the four-phased approach supports the reader to reflect on ethical considerations at every stage of the research process. This book is a welcome and essential resource that positions ethical perspectives at the heart of research activity with children.*"

Shirley Allen, Senior Lecturer Early Childhood Studies, Middlesex University, UK

"*This is an admirably clear and well-structured book that will be invaluable for anyone serious about research with children. The authors write from long experience, and provide a very helpful 'step by step' guide that is always underpinned by deeply principled, insightful considerations that exemplify good practice and respect for children. The use of real examples along with the authors' questions, invite the reader to reflect on their own thinking and actions, and the extensive checklists and sample documentation provide clear guidance that will be a valuable support for students and their supervisors, researchers, and practitioners alike. I look forward to making good use of this book in my own work and in my work with students of early childhood.*"

Sue Robson, Principal Lecturer, Subject Leader for Early Childhood Studies University of Roehampton, London, UK

"Doing Ethical Research with Children *is an invaluable resource for all student and practitioner-researchers who wish to honour children as active agents and significant voices in research. The book guides the reader through the processes of ethical research with (not on!) children, positioning the child as competent and capable. It includes practical guidance and examples of research so that issues that may emerge during a research project can be anticipated. My advice is – do not embark on an Early Years research project before reading it!*"

Lyn Trodd, Chair of the National Sector-Endorsed Foundation Degree in Early Years Network (SEFDEY), University of Hertfordshire, UK

Contents

List of figures and tables   x
Foreword   xi
About this book   xiv

1   **Research involving children**   1
     Introduction   1
     Why include children's perspectives in a research endeavour?   1
     Conceptualizing children and childhood   2
     Contemporary Euro-Western childhood   4
     Positions on research with children   6
     What then is ethical research?   10
     Your research questions   12
     Summary   13

2   **Phase 1 – preparing to research with children**   14
     Introduction   14
     Researcher predicaments   14
     Conceptualizing the project: including children's perspectives?   19
     International treaties and local laws   23
     Committing to the ethical and informed inclusion of children   28
     The researcher–participant relationship   30
     The balance of power between you and your participants   31
     Summary   35

3   **Building a research team: the Researcher Capacity Analysis**   36
     Introduction   36
     Skills   37
     Qualifications   38
     Experience   38
     Roles   39
     Training   39

The RCA in action   40
Summary   42
Phase 1 checklist   42

4 Phase 2 – research design   44
Introduction   44
The role of children in the research   44
Research design   45
Development of data collection tools   49
Sensitive subject matter   53
Recruitment   53
Ethical clearance from stakeholders/participants   54
Anonymity/confidentiality for the children   55
Ethics committees   57
Parents   61
Explanatory statements   61
Informed consent forms   63
Summary   64
Phase 2 checklist   64

5 Phase 3 – conducting the research   66
Opening the conversation: inviting children as research participants   66
Engaging with the children   69
Informed consent   70
Who will be invited   73
Extending the invitation   73
Documenting consent   74
Withdrawal of consent/opting out   77
Including all children   77
Researching across languages, cultures and unfamiliar contexts   79
Opening the research conversation   79
Summary   81

6 Maintaining ethical practice   82
Introduction   82
Ethical conduct   83
Including children in the analysis of data   86
Right to correction   88
Summary   89
Phase 3 checklist   89

7 Phase 4 – dissemination of your work   91
Introduction   91
Reporting back to the participants   92
A word on ethical presentation at conferences and seminars   93
Summary   94

Phase 4 checklist   95
Concluding remarks   95

Appendix 1   Over to You . . .   97
Appendix 2   **Researcher Capacity Analysis: individual**   100
             Researcher Capacity Analysis: project   101
Appendix 3   **Sample information letter to parents**   102
Appendix 4   **Sample letter of informed consent for parents**   104

References   105
Index   109

Figures and tables

Figures

5.1   Example of documented agreement 1   75
5.2   Example of documented agreement 2   76
5.3   Example of documented agreement 3   76

Tables

3.1   Researcher Capacity Analysis: individual   41
3.2   Researcher Capacity Analysis: project   41

Foreword

Children of all ages, in all cultures, know important things about life and the world. Their knowledge is based on experiences of love, trust and justice but also of dislike, disrespect and unfairness. Their views on human conditions are built on insights of the importance of power, be it a matter of economy, race, ethnicity, religion, gender or generation. Considering the wide range of life wisdom that children hold, it should seem obvious to involve them in research aiming at increasing our knowledge about life, relationships, society and other difficult and important human issues. However, until recently, such an idea was regarded as unexpected. Children's views and knowledge have been of interest primarily in the sense that they were held by young people on their way to *becoming* adults and their value as human beings was related to this fact. Important research agendas have been concerned with how to create, in as efficient ways as possible, support, control and assessment of children's developing abilities in order to prepare them for becoming complete adults in the future.

During recent decades, a dramatic shift away from this way of viewing children in policy, practice and research has taken place. This shift in perspective coincides with the international adoption and ratification of the United Nations (UN) Convention of the Rights of the Child, and also with the introduction of childhood studies at the end of the 1980s. Merging together, these two events have conveyed a moral and a scientific imperative, challenging taken-for-granted views on the child, children and childhood. From a research perspective research, a wide range of texts have been published, exploring what implications this repositioned view of the child may have for theoretical, methodological and ethical consideration.

Doing ethical research with children belongs to the field of literature where ethical implications of research *with* rather than *on* children are brought forward for discussion and reflection. However, this book brings us closer to concrete research practice, and its challenges, than many of its predecessors. In my reading of the text, I particularly appreciate the productive integration of distinguished phases in the research process, with the view of the child as the complex, competent and demanding human being now being referred to in contemporary policy, practice and research discourses.

Some key concepts to describe the contemporary child is worthy of mention here. First, we see the view of a child as a *subject*. Even though relationships with significant adults, such as parents and teachers, are very important for emerging insights and abilities about children and childhood, the child encounters the world on their own. Knowledge about what life is all about are formed through experiences, interpreted and made sense of by the child themself. For research, this means that the child carries knowledge that is not already known, by the researcher or by anyone else. In addition, this knowledge cannot be assessed or evaluated in pre-formulated checklists or tests. Viewing the child as a subject in this way means that we expect that the child has something to tell, something that is only available through their voice.

A second aspect is the child's right to *participate* and be involved in issues that concern them. This is about inviting the child as an equal party in dialogues that may lead to the establishment of, or change in, activities of interest for them. Being one of the main principles of the UN Convention, a child's participatory right has generally been under question, as it challenges a taken-for-granted power distribution between adults and children. Research is an activity through which life conditions for young human beings can be critically investigated and made visible. Viewing the child as someone who can, and indeed has the right to, contribute with important information calls for research strategies where the child is met with recognition and respect for what they have to tell.

A third concept concerns the child's *agency*, their competence and capacity to act independently, to make decisions and to express arguments and reasons that may go beyond or against the adult's interpretation of a problem or situation. The concept of agency may be a potential threat to adult power as it implicitly recognizes a child's ability and right to control and influence a situation. Consequently, viewing the child as having agency means that the researcher cannot solely control research processes. By inviting a child as a *participating subject with agency*, a certain amount of uncertainty must be inbuilt within planned and intended progress and outcomes of research. Alternative ways of doing and seeing may well be pointed out by the child as a participatory subject.

At a general principal level, the child as a participating subject, as summarized above, has been recognized in research. However, several difficult and complex ethical challenges have been discovered when rhetoric is turned into research practice. To a large extent the individual researcher is left alone in order to find strategies for how to invite the child to take part in a dialogue characterized by respect both for the child's ability to contribute information and, for being a subject with rights to control what, when and how this is to be done.

In *Doing ethical research with children* the authors have succeeded in maintaining the focus on the child throughout the research process. The book, therefore, is an excellent guide for supporting researchers with the motivation to take children's participatory rights in research seriously, particularly those who are in the beginning of their research experience. The authors describe research as a process over time, where ethical implications of inviting children to participate are continuously present. Ethical challenges and dilemmas likely to appear along the different phases of research are described, and steps for action are presented in systematic and concrete terms. The reoccurring invitations to the reader to pause the reading and to reflect upon their own thoughts on children, research and ethics, underline the dialogic character of the issue at hand.

I am convinced that *Doing ethical research with children* will serve as a perfect companion in planning and conducting research with children based on a view of the child as a respected project partner.

Professor Solveig Hägglund
Professor of Education and Head of Research
Karlstad University
Sweden

Member of the Scientific Council of Barnrättsakademin
(the Academy of Children's Rights)
Örebro University
Sweden

About this book

Doing ethical research with children is intended to support you in developing, conducting and disseminating research matters relating to children and childhood with an ethical imperative. This book should assist you, the researcher, to focus and identify many of the key issues surrounding research with children. It presents an overview of the contemporary and traditional perspectives relating to child-related research practices.

This book combines relevant theoretical and practical information in a format that should act as a guide for engaging with the issues and essential elements for conducting ethical research with children. In this way, you will not only consider these elements, but also be prompted to systematically address them. The reflection activities within each section assume the philosophical position of the child as a competent and capable contributor to research endeavours. This guide will assist you in positioning your research so that it values, respects, identifies and enables children's authentic and ethical participation in research.

This book is therefore intended to act as both a guide and reflection tool in order to assist researchers with the unique considerations for research involving children. By undertaking sustained consideration to the ethical deliberations within any project that involves children, you are more likely to identify and address these aspects faithfully throughout the life of the project. This text does not pretend to ask all the questions, nor provide all of the answers. However, it should serve to encourage, in each researcher, a greater awareness of the range of considerations for conducting ethical research involving children. Even the most well-prepared research projects rarely proceed neatly from preparation to publication without ethical hiccups.

Doing ethical research with children is presented using a four-phased approach. We have decided that separating the research process into discrete segments will achieve two key objectives. First, it will assist you in developing a strategic approach to the development and conduct of your project. By focusing on the important aspects of each phase you can give the most appropriate attention to the procedure, strategies and project concentration that each phase needs for a successful outcome. Second, and in our view the critical reason for identifying key phases of the research project, is because each phase presents distinct ethical considerations for you as the researcher.

Throughout all research there are essential elements of progression and refinement. The natural and logical forward movement through a project is dependent on the success of the previous steps. So, too, when considering the involvement of children in a research endeavour. A researcher's perspective, understanding and deliberations of the role/s of children in their project will also progress. To maintain a focus on the ethical aspects of doing research with children, the participation of children should be thoughtfully considered, challenged and reflected upon at each phase of the project. Children in research should not be a 'set and forget' element of the process. Unfortunately, until very recently, many projects that involved children had the tendency to assume that once parental consent had been obtained, child agreement to participate was also obtained. This guide begins at the conceptualization of a project and seeks to hold the position of children at the forefront throughout *every* phase of the research.

As an organizer guide for initiating and completing a successful project, the following four phases have been identified: Preparing to research (Phase 1), Research design (Phase 2), Conducting the research (Phase 3) and Disseminating the research (Phase 4). Each phase has a particular focus which presents many opportunities for reflection. To assist you in unpacking these considerations, we provide some reflection activities around common issues that may arise. As the Phase names suggest, this book begins with strategic thinking and reflection about the project and the ethics of involving children (Phases 1 and 2). It then moves to strategic action (Phases 3 and 4) where the considerations and objectives of the project are put into practice, thereby honouring the ethical inclusion of children.

Phase 1 explores a range of contemporary views about the broader issues and theoretical standpoints surrounding children and childhood. How and why children are being included (or not) in research are highlighted. We present some dilemmas for reflection in an attempt to assist you in identifying how you currently view children and childhood. The exploring and understanding the particular views of children that you bring to the project is critical to your conceptualization of an ethical approach to research with children. The extent and merits of including children in the project itself are examined.

Phase 2 builds on the insights gained in Phase 1 and discusses the most appropriate research activities that involve children. An exploration of issues that impact children are offered, which should inform the development of credible and worthwhile research questions. This phase also guides you through a self-audit of your own capacity to conduct a particular project while maintaining an ethical approach.

Phase 3 explores the movement from project design and skill development to the practical aspects of the project. This focus considers how ethical intentions and understanding can be put into practice while considering the unpredictable nature of field-based research. The involvement of children during Phase 3 of a project is at its most substantial. As such, the key elements of informed consent and ongoing communication with children are at the core of this section.

Phase 4 discusses the dissemination of the research to the wider community and to the children themselves. Confidentiality and honouring the key intentions of the children and concluding the project are the focus.

Throughout the book there are many opportunities for reflection, discussion and deliberation so that by your project's end you can be confident that to the best of your ability and intention, you will have undertaken ethical research with children and are well prepared to repeat such a research endeavour.

We wish you all the very best with your work with children.

Jonathon Sargeant and Deborah Harcourt

1

Research involving children

Introduction

The conduct of timely, ethical and reliable research in matters affecting children is of mounting importance in contemporary research communities. Alongside this recognition is a growing acknowledgement of children's rights and agency within research methodologies. The inclusion of children's perspectives is being understood as a critical consideration when preparing any child-related research and beneficial at all stages of the research endeavour. However, until quite recently many studies relating to children were often directed solely by adults and their particular adult-determined themes. These studies have seldom reflected on, or even considered, the research process from the child perspective.

This chapter introduces the notion of research with children and seeks to guide you through a reflexive process that will assist in formulating a clear philosophical foundation for developing your research agenda. This agenda should be grounded in an acknowledgement and appreciation of the contributions children can make to high-quality research should they be empowered to do so. As a researcher with an interest in matters affecting children and young people, you should be clear in your conceptualizations, understandings and knowledge of children and childhood. This chapter begins with and hopefully builds on the understandings you already have, thereby enhancing your research activities.

Why include children's perspectives in a research endeavour?

Since the beginning of this century, the sociology of childhood (Mayall 2002) has guided the conceptualization of children as active and competent *beings* and continues to offer insights into our current understanding about children and childhood. Pivotal to Mayall's theory, which underpins much research with children, is an acknowledge-ment that the presence of children and their accounts of their own experiences is an essential element in understanding their lifeworlds (Rinaldi 2006). The sociology of childhood's acknowledgement of children's competence assists us in exploring how children learn, how they mature, their processes of cognitive and emotional development, and their place in the world as influenced by their environment (Prasad 2002; Archard 2004). This sociological conceptualization challenges many of the traditional and popular notions of defined and predetermined transitions through the human lifespan as described in developmental psychology. Rather than simply accepting that children grow to *become* an adult, it positions children as competent social actors, *being*, in their own right.

The question of why include children's perspectives in research can attract a range of responses that reflect the often polarized views of children and their capacities. Attitudes of suspicion towards children's capacities remain widespread. As Thomson (2007) points out, children's views are often perceived as simply a learned or parroted response particularly if you subscribe to the notion that 'you listen to children and you hear their parents' voices'. However, the growing body of evidence that demonstrates the child as a reliable actor across the entire research process refutes long-held notions that children, simply by virtue of their age, cannot provide reliable information that can assist researchers in doing their work (Dockett and Perry 2003). For many years the child's voice has been left silent and, as such, researchers need to explore their own prejudice and cultural memory when working with children. The adult-centred assumptions that children are simply adults-in-waiting, something they are clearly not, must be challenged.

Thomson (2007: 208) argues, 'the key question is not whether we should listen to children but how best to represent this group's many voices'. By willingly increasing their participation as co-researchers and research advisers alongside adult researchers, children between birth and 18 years of age have an opportunity for a shared agency in research enterprises that can make visible children's views and opinions (Fattore *et al.* 2007). This process begins with a strong conceptualization of children and childhood beyond the restrictive designations of age and maturity.

Conceptualizing children and childhood

In any study involving children, it is important to be clear and consistent when referring to your participants and their roles. However, the terms 'children' and 'childhood' can be described in many ways and certain fields of study follow specific conventions. By establishing some clear definitions of your focus participants, children, you will be better prepared to position your research team with a well-defined purpose and plan. Clearly articulating *who the children are* that you intend to conduct research with, will assist you in planning, conducting and communicating the results of your study.

Terms such as 'young child', 'child', 'adolescent' and 'young people' all mean different things to different people. It is important to define and maintain the same terminology throughout your documentation so as to remain coherent, not only in your communication, but also in your thinking. By noting early on in the process how you personally define many of the interchangeable labels placed on children, you will be better equipped to maintain focus throughout the key processes of the project: question development, literature review, design, conduct and dissemination. As a beginning point, note your current definitions in the boxes below. These definitions may develop or change as you progress, but it may be important later, to identify where you began.

Over to you . . .

What boundaries or definitions do you place on the following terms?

- Children

- Young children

- Kids

- Tweens

- Youth

- Teenagers

- Young people

- Adolescents

The difficulties in developing a common definition of childhood, combined with adult presumptions of the capacities of children, means that many contradictory views of children and childhood continue (UNICEF 2004). As such, conceptions of children and childhood continue to be portrayed according to different criteria. By its very nature childhood is an identifiable and distinct stage of a person's life that has always been socially constructed, changing as societies change (Jamrozik and Sweeney 1996). The ever-increasing influence of the media, and the 24-hour news cycle, has heightened many communities' awareness of the potential dangers threatening children. With this increased awareness comes an intensified emphasis by professionals to act according to what *they* consider to be in the child's best interests. As well intentioned as these actions may be, the views and wishes of children have remained largely ignored (Valentine 1999). Similarly, Grover (2004: 91) stated: 'it is time that children are regarded as experts on their own subjective experience'.

Within the emerging contemporary social constructions of childhood there is a rising emphasis on creating child-friendly communities with provisions for children as empowered community members in their own right. These emerging critical perspectives enable adults to better provide for children, sustain their development, protect them and prepare them for their futures. To further achieve this, Cook-Sather (2002) suggests a reconfiguration of the power dynamics between adults and children so that new forums are created where children can exercise their political rights to speak out.

A sticking point in this development sits with the varying conceptualizations of the individual *child* compared with *children* as a collective and their positioning within a time in life defined as *childhood*. Before the full recognition and inclusion of children's capacities can be enacted in research, individual researchers such as yourself must first consider your own existing definitions of the child, children and childhood, both personally and professionally. By reflecting on your own understandings of the extent to which you currently position children as capable and knowledgeable on matters affecting them, so you will be better prepared to engage in research that is both inclusive and ethical.

Over to you . . .

How do you conceptualize the following 'stages' of childhood?

- Early years

- Middle years

- Adolescence

Contemporary Euro-Western childhood

While each child and stage of childhood is unique, in many aspects of childhood, children share a number of commonalities. In each context, the most common features for Euro-Western societies include a life under a particular set of protections, laws and school systems. The increasing automaticity of Euro-Western communities today offers a situation where children do not need to learn manual skills for survival. In fact, the development of cognitive functions and skills to enhance technological freedoms for the community has become a priority. In this technological age, computers, the Internet, and television are presented as central to daily learning.

Many children today live in a constructed and technological age where entertainment, education and domestic life are determined by their family's socio-economic circumstances. In numerous contemporary societies children learn from an early age to accumulate and are being provided with modern devices intended to make life more comfortable. Many children have access to television, computers, the Internet and mobile devices, both at home and at school. More children now commute to and from school by private transport than in recent generations and young children are now rarely seen in local areas and playgrounds without adult supervision.

Some commentators conceptualize childhood as a natural and gradual progression through the early years, the middle years, adolescence and then on to adulthood. In childhood, your world is your own. They suggest, that the wisdom, experience and knowledge of the adult world is passed on to you in a way that is intended as most beneficial to your development but is dependent on the perceived level of capacity you have at a particular age.

For many, the idealized view of a carefree childhood represents their conceptualization of what childhood is and should be. However, there also exists an alternative, less positive view of children's development, one that is more worryingly influenced by modern issues. This view suggests that children observe the adult world as undesirable and representative of a very pessimistic outlook on the future. It is these negative features of a perceived adult world that researchers suggest weigh heavily on children particularly if children's expectations of the future directly impact on their function as a child (Simpson 2004).

The modern Euro-Western child also lives a very restricted life. Children have few opportunities to act on their own behalf except in the social domain, where they can exercise some autonomy through interactions with their peers. In many countries the child remains not only protected but also restricted by law until they are 18 years old. The child it could be said is free to be carefree, yet the carefree childhood is one determined largely at the will of adults.

In ancient times, children were taught their 'adult' role at a young age (Muller 1969). In some cultures, the women would do all work to ensure the comfort of the men, while the men's role as leader and protector of the community was paramount. These core community values were instilled in children at a very early age; childhood was 'hard work' (Muller 1969; Morss 1990; Furedi 2001; Gidley and Inayatullah 2002). The notion that a child must grow in safety and relative freedom is flawed in that this situation has probably never existed. If it did, it has only been of prevalence in the last 50 years coinciding with unprecedented technological advances and Western wealth accumulation.

In reality, children have never lived in a domain that is completely carefree, and for many, modern childhood is also not viewed as being in a child's best interests. Such a view places pressure on the community to protect children across the breadth of activities and experiences available to children, in their best interests. A consequence of this is the reduction in basic freedoms afforded to children. The effect of this, from the child's perspective, is not well known.

Much of childhood is seemly experienced in plain sight of adults and often played out and debated through the media. Children, however, also assume a range of 'under the radar lives' as determined by the context in which they are involved. Children act differently and adhere to different social rules within their various guises be it their school life, their home life or their (secret) social media life. In order to understand the complexity of childhood, many of these factors must be considered. Yet from an adult perspective, judgements are often made based on the most visible points of reference. Formulating such judgements without including the perspectives of the children can lead to conflict and disjunction between the lived and the observed.

Recent research that includes children's perspectives reveals that children are being switched on to the knowledge of the adult world earlier in life (Sargeant 2010). Consequently, children's ability and the ability of influential adults (teachers/parents) to encourage and foster the ideal carefree childhood may be impeded (Langeveld 2003). For some children, exposure to real-world issues is forced upon them; that is, viewing the images of the victims of natural disasters, extreme poverty or civil/political unrest. For the majority of children in the Euro-Western world, these events are a rare occurrence. However, with the pervasiveness of the media and other information sources, these events not directly impacting on children's lives may still have a durable effect.

Each child lives under a various set of circumstances including the size and constitution of their family, varying levels of wealth and security and other demographic features relating to their local context. Because of these and other influences, there are limitations to the extent childhood or any particular feature of childhood can be categorized by adults (Prout 2005). It is, however, possible to gain an understanding of the essence of a child's world by conducting research that includes their perspective (Minichiello 1999).

Researchers, who hold a view of the child as capable experts in their own world, seek the active and informed participation of the individual child. They view the child as a full but developing human with rights and responsibilities, an individual that has an interest in both the present and the future. However, adults' views of the child seem to be constantly changing as the contexts in which children are observed, discussed or interacted with also change.

Without discounting the individuality of each child, nor oversimplifying the commonalities, studies that seek to investigate the perspectives of children as they are offered to (not as created by) the researcher, generate a rich contribution to our understandings that represents an authentic and ethical account of children's life worlds.

As much as we already know about children and childhood, further research is necessary as this important stage of life continues to evolve and mystify. Regardless of the views held about contemporary childhood it remains clear that children should be consulted prior to regulating, standardizing and studying their lives (Prout 2005). How children/childhood are conceptualized from the very beginning of a research endeavour will determine the ease of, or barriers, to effective and ethical consideration during the project. Underrating the capacities of children, and/or overrating the adults' capacities, ignores the potentially significant insights into the social, emotional, physical, political and educational requirements of children and childhood.

Over to you . . .

We have presented some commentary on a Euro-Western perspective of contemporary childhood. What other perspectives do you envisage exist about childhood in non-Euro-Western thinking?

Positions on research with children

As your perspectives and conceptualizations of children and childhood continue to take shape, so too will your perspective of how children can and should be included in research endeavour. Therefore, not only is it important that you are clear with your own view of children and childhood, but also that you consider how your perspectives will inform your philosophical position on the act of researching with children. Your conceptualizations of children will influence your thinking, your methods and possibly your analysis of the data. Understanding the compatibility between your perspectives and your research methodology is critical to research success. Three key philosophies/traditions often shape projects that involve children; the hermeneutic philosophy, face value or phenomenological research and the experimental or scientific tradition of research are discussed briefly in the following section.

Researcher views of research with children

The process of reflecting on children and childhood has merit in itself, as you develop an agenda of research activity that may involve children or relate to issues affecting children. When representing a standpoint on children, adults draw upon the interplay between the various perspectives that are informed by the research context. A researcher's understanding of 'child', 'children' or 'childhood' is interpreted within the relational context (e.g. student, sibling, offspring), the physical context (e.g. home, at school, in public) and/or the situational context (e.g. bullying, studying, socializing) to form a conceptualization of what 'a child' is to them for that particular research purpose.

Having identified your own perspectives on the notion of the individual child, now turn your attention to children more broadly. As we have suggested, notions of modern childhood and its stages, standing and duration are matters of continued debate in many societies. While contemporary impressions of childhood have their origins in the sixteenth century (Aries 1962), much of the current debate centres on the interpretations of childhood as a time of being, becoming or a combination of both. We have noted how these varying perspectives are being compounded by the rapidly evolving information age of the twenty-first century that offer children access to more unregulated information from multiple sources than at any time in history. As such, the adult community is confronted by a conundrum. Do they prepare children for their future lives as adults by equipping them with information management skills? Or alternatively, do they seek to preserve childhood as a time defined by freedom and carefree living, protecting children from the dangers of media exposure, unsafe behaviour and societal immorality (Jans 2004; Sargeant 2005, 2007)?

Within the range of protections, provisions and considerations afforded to children and childhood, their roles and capacities remain contested. Whether developmental or sociological perspectives inform these conceptualizations, the notion of childhood itself is difficult to define due to the number of variables and factors that influence its construction. As King (2007: 196) notes:

> There is no definitive or universal account of what childhood is or what children should be. All is relative and depends upon the particular constructions of childhood of different societies or of the same society at different times and the expectations associated with children (and adults) resulting from these constructions.

Childhood is often conceptualized across domains such as competence, capacity, ability, vulnerability and age. Historically, children have often been seen as innocent, fragile and in need of protection. Children have been viewed as becoming and in need of guidance towards adult capacity and, until achieved, requiring firm control and discipline (Saraga 1998). When considering research with children there is a perceived and often assumed authority that the adult brings to the context. The notion of the 'child' must be separated from the notion of 'children' yet this is an almost impossible task.

Over to you . . .

How does your definition of child sit with your definition of children? How does this then relate to your definition of contemporary childhood? From which 'view' will you position children in your project?

A hermeneutic view of research with children

Children express themselves in many ways. In many respects the 'language' of children and childhood is just that, a language, which must be translated, interpreted and contextualized before its true meaning is revealed. Much of the research that involves children requires careful engagement with a range of childhood languages including oral, text, artefacts and behaviour that are often foreign to the adult researcher. Research that involves children is often *hermeneutic* in character in that hermeneutics is often referred to as the art of interpretation (Dowling 2004). In practice, hermeneutics is the reading, the interpretation, of messages and texts. In research, the world of the child is experienced through the interpretation of their language in all its forms. By engaging with the child's world hermeneutically, language provides both understanding and knowledge (Dowling 2004). Any text must be read to make sense, but one must first know the language in which it is constructed; in this case the language of the child. Understanding the text/context relationship is crucial to research that involves children (Packer and Addison 1989). Knowledge gained within a hermeneutic framework is not achieved through the stringent adherence to a doctrine of collection and analysis but rather the 'illumination of the ordinary process of understanding' (Dowling 2004: 32).

A key principle in hermeneutics is the acknowledgement of your role as the researcher within the context of the study. The development of the research project and subsequent research questions are borne out of a perception and particular view of the world held by the researcher. You bring to the study a number of preconceptions formed from personal experience and knowledge that cannot be ignored or easily factored out of the research design. As Blacker (1993: 2) states 'the interpretive challenge is to maintain simultaneously the attitude of openness toward the text or person while also permitting, as best one can, one's own prejudices to rise to the surface so as to put them in to play'. By understanding and acknowledging the influences and notions already held by the researcher, the data that emerge have even greater richness.

A face value view of research with children

Within the context of many child-related studies, it is the concept of 'face value' (Cohen *et al.* 2007) that is most important to research. Such research is not searching for particular themes nor seeking to discount themes that are unattractive to the researcher. A key feature of phenomenology, face value research affords weight to the emergent themes based on the information presented by each child. No judgement is made about the intellectual or experiential capacity of the child to produce a valid response. In achieving this, data is analysed as a discrete response without consideration of variables such as age or gender.

The face value approach is achieved by acknowledging the anonymity of each child to you, the researcher. This is an important consideration when no personal contact is made between you and the child either before or after a study is conducted. These studies, and there are many that fit such a criteria, leave the researcher with no option but to consider their data as complete and discrete. By doing so you may assume that when a child speaks the child actually means what they say and report it as such (Cruddas 2006).

However, it is equally important to consider whether a child is always saying what they mean. If we take the child's voice at face value and transcribe literally, we may not always be getting the message that is actually intended by the child. Due to reasons of language construction or a limited experience, children sometimes speak their thoughts out loud as a way of organizing their ideas. These utterances do not necessarily represent the complete perspectives of the child, but are more representative of the process of think-aloud problem-solving. The adult researcher may be hearing a series of deliberations rather than an absolute conclusion presented by the child. As researcher if you do not understand this, the literal interpretation of what the children are saying may be misrepresented in your research communications. The most effective way to include children ethically in research is in facilitating what Parsons (2003: 64) calls 'shared authority' in acknowledging what children are thinking and feeling and seeking clarification directly from the children when required. By affording attention to children's cognitive and emotional capacities, children may be more likely to engage willingly and authentically in the research process.

An experimental view of research with children

An experimental or positivist view of research is guided by four key principles: determinism, empiricism, parsimony and generality (Cohen *et al.* 2007). Determinism works on the assumption that all events and behaviours have an underlying cause that can be systematically uncovered and understood. Empiricism assumes that any event, its cause and effect can be verified through observation and experience. Parsimony seeks to explain the behaviours in the simplest way possible. Generality is the principle of relating research findings to explain the wider context or population. When considering research with children, applying an experimental design presents some significant challenges. The application of an experimental approach in real-world settings such as a child's school is difficult, and often inappropriate due to the huge number of variables that are out of your control. The context of the child's home and school environment has many elements that go far beyond what would be considered manageable. For example, when describing the features of the regular classroom, Doyle (1986) categorized these variables as publicness, multidimensionality, simultaneity, history, unpredictability and immediacy, emphasizing their combined influence on classroom cohesion. In fact, any attempts to control these elements would place the research itself at risk of bias if not correctly acknowledged.

In naturalistic settings such as classrooms, a qualitative approach is usually most appropriate. In many studies, the genuine influences in a child's life and their ongoing effects are of interest to research. They will vary from child to child in a way that is not easily measurable. Within a qualitative framework, research that is not as constrained by constructed parameters allows themes to emerge from the data in the analysis rather than being sought after according to specific preset criteria.

In seeking the views of young children, ethical research does not seek to evaluate or define children's attitudes, but tends to reflect upon and consider the essence of what children are saying. It cannot be assumed that every person is the same or that they participate in an activity for the same reason or from the same perspectives, applies that same knowledge, or has the same experience. As such, experimental norms and processes cannot be reasonably employed in many socialized settings such as schools. If only for these reasons, qualitative investigations must be undertaken within a structure considered trustworthy in its contributions to knowledge (Denzin and Lincoln 2000).

What then is ethical research?

Ethics in the context of this book can be described as a moral code of practice that guides a researcher throughout the process of conducting a study. Engaging in acceptable researcher behaviour must be a priority in any research endeavour. A number of norms of conduct that are learned, developed and practised by the researcher will assist in achieving this aim. Any research that involves humans, and in particular children, requires a knowledge and understanding of what constitutes ethical behaviour. There are clear ethical rules governing the conduct of a study that if breached would constitute misconduct and may lead to legal sanction. These rules and procedures are clearly stipulated in the main processes outlined by universities and other authorizing bodies that oversee research activity. These rules actively seek to protect under law the participants, the researcher and the research institution. Such processes may include recruitment, consent, coercion, fabrication of results and plagiarism and often fall under the expression 'research integrity'.

Another element of ethical research that may not constitute formal misconduct or attract legal sanction exists in the context of research with children. The Australian National Statement on Ethical Conduct in Research (Australian Government 2007: 2) states that: '"Ethical conduct in human research" is therefore oriented to something more fundamental than ethical "do's" and "don'ts" – namely, an ethos that should permeate the way those engaged in human research approach all that they do in their research'.

While you may consider yourself highly ethical in your research practice and understand clearly the difference between right and wrong, many grey areas of practice can arise in the process of a study. Unethical practice can occur as a result of inexperience, practical mistakes, poor data collection, inappropriate interactions or ineffective monitoring of the research site. Many of these errors can occur unintentionally and, in fact, many researchers are often oblivious to the possibility that their research involving children could be considered unethical.

Beyond the legal considerations, researching ethically with children will take practice, knowledge and require a great deal of reflection. Research practice is influenced by many factors including an understating of the roles and influences of the participants, the environment and the research procedures. Minor changes or mis-interpretations of any of these during the research process may result in actions that are not ethically sound, yet legal.

You would never fabricate results, falsify data or plagiarize, all of which are highly unethical. However, you may not realize that by offering the participants a reward, for example, a chocolate bar for answering your questions could constitute an inducement to participate. You may also not realize that taking photos and publishing them as illustrations of children's play behaviour (without their prior consent), even if the children cannot be readily identified in the picture, is in fact unethical. Deviations from ethical conduct can and does occur in research, often as a result of ignorance or as a failure to reflect critically on the process. By considering these 'softer' aspects of ethical research with children prior to conducting the study can achieve two key outcomes. First, you can reduce the incidence of serious deviations by improving your understanding of ethics and being sensitized to the potential issues that can arise. Second, the study itself can provide a model for authentic engagement with children in order to achieve more positive research outcomes.

Ponder this . . .

Gérard, a child psychologist, was interested in documenting the views of children who were suffering chronic illness. He was particularly keen on listening to children who experienced long-term hospitalization and medical intervention. His view was that the hospital system was having a negative influence on children and that changes effected to date were having little positive impact on children's well-being. Over a three-month period, Gérard attempted to have meaningful research conversations with children ranging in age from 6 to 17 years. While many children seemed willing to hear him out as he described his project, most children told him they were tired of talking to doctors. While he tried to convince the children he was not a medical doctor, only three out of a potential research cohort of 36 children actually engaged in discussions. Gérard was very disappointed as he thought children's views would be so beneficial to making changes to the system, but no amount of coercion, even when offering iTunes vouchers, worked for him.

When considering the child as an active participant in research, more questions arise. Children may sometimes choose not to participate even against what you believe is in their best interests, simply because they do not want to be involved. If the child believes your research is worth while and probably more importantly, interesting, they are likely to agree to participate. However, some children might believe the research is worth while but do not want to be involved. Regardless of parental consent and other approval processes, must the child's wishes be respected at every stage of the project, even if the project will directly benefit the child being studied? What if the project will save their life? How do you ethically honour their wishes against what you believe is in their interests?

A researcher facing an ethical dilemma must make a decision and then take action. Planning ahead can reduce the likelihood of a dilemma arising but if it does, the researcher is going to need to be prepared to recognize the dilemma and respond appropriately. You may decide to ask more questions, gather more information, explore different options, or consider other ethical rules. Whatever the decision, you must be able to justify your decision to yourself, as well as to colleagues, administrators and other people who might be affected. You should be able to articulate reasons for your conduct from an ethical perspective. In other words, you should be able to recognize and defend that what you are doing is ethically the right thing to do regardless of the effect on the study. Would your actions stand up to further publicity and scrutiny? Could you live with it? Is your decision just, fair and responsible?

Your research questions

Research that seeks children's own accounts of their life worlds and their lived experiences of the services and communities in which they participate offers a unique contribution to our understandings of childhood and the position of children as active and participatory agents in society. Such research can open our eyes to children's competence and capacities. It also brings our attention to children's disempowered role in the wider community where their perspectives are infrequently sought.

Ponder this . . .

Phoebe decided to brainstorm some possible research questions with her Master's students. She asked them to consider what would be appropriate questions that would indicate to the thesis examiners that their project was clearly situated within the framework of 'research with children'. These are some of the ideas offered by the students:

- How does the notion of student engagement replicate the rhetoric in the Swedish National Curriculum?
- In what ways are secondary school students involved in cyber bullying?
- What impact does teacher efficacy have on young children's social development?
- How are children and young people involved in consent procedures for medical interventions?
- What are young children's standpoints of the quality of their preschool experiences?
- How do teenagers relate to a non-custodial parent in times of personal upheaval?
- What are the concerns of Year 6 children who are about to transit into secondary school?

While it is not the focus of this book to prescribe the development of your research topic or questions, it is appropriate at this stage for you to reflect on what you have done so far. You will have:

- identified a topic area
- conceptualized or positioned your project within the framework of research with children
- carefully considered in what way and how children will be central to the study.

We now come to your research questions. Your main research question is the key reference point that will sustain your entire project and should be reasonably certain as early as possible. As your project develops, further sub-questions may emerge that will guide your study and this group of questions will become the critical focus for your entire project. As we leave this chapter and prepare for the next, we ask you to document your thinking here.

Over to you . . .

- **What are your key research questions?**

- **How do your research questions relate to how you see children and childhood?**

Summary

This chapter has focused on:

- constructing a critical rationale for ethical research with children;
- the varying historical and contemporary of conceptualizations of children and childhood;
- an exploration of contemporary childhoods and the key influences on children in the Euro-Western context;
- the common philosophies and traditions that positions research with children;
- a discussion of the key principles of what constitutes ethical research;
- the focused and principled development of your research questions.

2
Phase 1 – preparing to research with children

Introduction

Having considered the discussions and focused your thinking through the reflexive activities in Chapter 1, you should now have a clearer understanding of your own philosophical position on the roles, capacities and attributes of children and childhood in your field of interest.

This chapter focuses on guiding you through a process of conceptualizing an ethical research project that includes children. The discussion now extends to support researchers in making the link between theoretical positions and the necessary ethical and practical considerations *prior* to designing a research project. We challenge researchers to consider how particular views of children and childhood may influence project design. As with Chapter 1, this chapter provides pivotal ideas for critical reflection and self-assessment that focuses on your capacity to engage in research from an ethical and practical perspective.

From this point on your continuing reflections and preparation for research is informed by your responses and thinking developed in Chapter 1. The recurrent questions relating to authentic and ethical research that arise throughout the development and implementation of a research project are more likely to be effectively addressed within a context of enhanced understanding of the issues and dilemmas of child-focused research. Many questions can emerge through the journey of a research endeavour. We address these in more detail throughout the following sections of this book, but at this point it is worth looking at some of the key issues that are most relevant to the preparatory phase of your project.

Researcher predicaments

We now offer some discussion of the key issues and considerations researchers face when preparing a research project outside of the core research questions. Successfully addressing these matters early in the process will assist in the smooth conduct of the research proper. While some of these issues will not directly affect the project itself, they are important for contextualizing the study and may assist in the design and theoretical development across the project.

How will your study impact/improve the children's lifeworlds?

In preparing a project it is important to consider the direct impact your involvement will have on the children in your study. Even the least intrusive of studies can have some indirect or lasting effect on the participants. If your study involves face-to-face interactions or observations of children in naturalistic settings, it should be recognized that over time a relationship will develop between you and the children.

While your study may indeed only have minimal impact on the children, they should always be informed and reminded when appropriate that your involvement will be temporary. This explanation should be provided to the children prior to the study's commencement. In addition it is wise to plan for your exit from the children's setting at the conclusion of the study so that this transition is smooth for all concerned. A planned exit strategy that includes how you will communicate to the children regarding your future departure is particularly important if your study involves repeated or frequent interactions.

What are the key characteristics of the children in your study?

The children you are seeking to include (or exclude) from your study will impact on many aspects of your project. The key demographics you are seeking will be informed by the nature of your research question, the research methodology, literature review, data collection instruments and intended analytical processes. These features will also inform the choice of location, duration and assistance required in collecting the data. These elements are discussed in detail later when we look at the Researcher Capacity Analysis, as the success of the project can be shaped by these factors, whether individually or collectively.

Ponder this . . .

Pene was concerned that the government was pursuing an agenda around moving children who are in Grade 7, currently the last year of primary (elementary) school, into secondary schools. This has been decided through a consultative process including teachers, academics, community and parents. However, Pene notes that current and future Grade 7 children have not been consulted, and therefore their voice has been silenced. Her research question therefore is 'How do current Grade 6 and 7 students view the move of Grade 7 into secondary schools?' She wishes to gather a representative view of children in order to add to the broader conversation on this decision, and therefore needs to makes some decisions about demographics.

Demographics

When identifying who you will invite to be involved in your study, it is important to carefully examine your research question. At all times, the study should be guided by the knowledge you are seeking to advance rather than what is most easily achieved. The identification of specific populations of children should be a secondary concern. Those who you invite should represent the children most broadly appropriate to your study.

Understanding the key characteristics of your participants is essential in ensuring that the appropriate support and level of expertise is available to maintain the children's authentic inclusion. You should also be aware of any unique issues or characteristic of individuals that need to be considered prior to the project's implementation. Such an analysis should not be undertaken in order to *exclude* any particular group of children, but should confirm for you that any particular group's inclusion is a necessity and in their best interests to be involved.

An example of such a group might be children from a particular socio-economic group who have regularly been included in research projects. These children may be overexposed to research projects, because of their circumstances, and may be tired of constantly being investigated. It is also probable that they have not personally been involved in the development of the projects or directly benefited from the results of previous studies. In many cases, the results are not shared with the participants after a study is complete. As a result, these children may be cautious about further research that is not explicitly relevant to their own context. As a researcher wishing to invite groups of children such as those who might be 'over-researched', it is essential that you carefully think through the process for communicating the reasons for your study and how the results will be communicated to the children.

> **Over to you . . .**
>
> Two key questions you might ask yourself at this stage are:
>
> 1 Is the intrusion into these children's lives essential to the success of my study?
>
> 2 How will I demonstrate that the research outcomes will improve their lifeworlds?

Age

The age of the children to be included is of importance when developing the study. Your understanding of the impact of a child's age should be informed by your conceptualizations as developed in Chapter 1. Again, however, it is central that the age of the children involved becomes a consideration only after the research question has been developed. International treaties such as the United Nations Convention on the Rights of the Child (UNCRC), which is discussed later, assures children of their right to express their views, which is not dependent on their competence to express a mature view; rather, that they have the competence to form and express a view (Lundy 2007). That is, the child's view is commensurate with the child's age and maturity; it is not dependent on it.

Having a general interest in a particular age group is not grounds for developing a research project, unless it is something that is age specific such as 'How do young children view turning five?' or the reflection activity given earlier about Grades 6 and 7 children. At each stage of childhood, from the very early years through to the later years of adolescence, children bring unique language, behaviour and knowledge to a research project that requires careful thinking. The chosen materials, explanatory statements, data collection methods and communication techniques should reflect the participants' demonstrated capacity. These capacities will vary within and across an age range and may require some refinement during the project, but a detailed and thoughtful understanding of the target group should occur in advance. Of particular importance in relation to age is in explaining the project and inviting children's participation in a medium they will understand.

Community context

Other factors that you will need to consider in terms of your participants include children who are speakers of other languages, children with special needs and diverse abilities, children from different cultural or religious backgrounds, children from low socio-economic status families or children who have found themselves or are members of a marginalized group. Gender may also be a consideration, as may be your own, within the context of the project. We discuss issues of power and the relationship-building process required later, but it is relevant to mention here that an understanding of some of the key differences between boys and girls may affect your work. There is a plethora of research on this subject, which, if appropriate, you should consult in advance.

In addition, children in care or from non-traditional family groups may be present in your study. You will know some of these factors from the beginning; other information may come to your attention during the project, while other material you may never discover. If you are, or become aware of these factors, it may be helpful to gain some further information from professional organizations if you feel you need further assistance in supporting these children from the perspective of being involved in your project. If children disclose any of their personal circumstances to you, it is important to remain sensitive to their position. You may not need to respond or act upon the information they provide, but your knowledge of their particular situation may affect some of your work. It is most important to remain sensitive to the potential for children experiencing difficult life circumstances who may be working with you. At all times, throughout your work, you need to remain aware so that even children who you know and discover little about feel at ease during their involvement.

Ponder this . . .

Ole was very interested in examining Swedish children's construction of human rights from the viewpoint of multiple ages and life experiences. He thought he might have research conversations with preschoolers, and children in Years

2, 5, 9 and 12 as he felt this would give him a broad representation. He also wanted to include children of the Sami people, as he knew indigenous issues were important, and some of the unaccompanied minors from Albania who had just started at the local school because of his keen interest in social justice. Ole's research supervisor was not sure that Ole had the skill base necessary to collect data from such a broad range of ages and contexts. She has asked Ole to hand in a proposal for data collection to outline his thinking around this matter. Ole was sure he had it all under control.

Considerations in researching with your chosen cohort of children

Even the most well-prepared research projects are likely to encounter some challenges. Many of these are detailed through this book but we ask you to take some time to consider some of the possible hurdles you might confront. For example, the children and other participants might not respond to your data collection methods in the way anticipated. They might have agreed to be involved in your study but lose interest because they simply do not have the same level of passion for your topic that you do. In this case you may have to reconsider how you can refine the project so it is more relevant and interesting to the children. A thick skin is particularly useful if you do receive some negative feedback! Reflect for a moment on how you might react to these kinds of situation. Is your response likely to help or hinder the relationship you are trying to build?

Two other not so obvious challenges that may arise include:

- The behaviour of the children when working with you in the absence of their regular authority figures such as teachers or parents. This may change from session to session and can be difficult to predict with children of any age.

- The mood of the children on any given day. Mood is quite different to behaviour, which are the externalized actions of the children. A child's (and sometimes your own) mood will generally fluctuate and can influence the level and depth of responses particularly in focus group or interviews. Whatever it is that caused the mood, whether excited or melancholic may also influence the nature of the children's responses. Depending on your project focus, this may be a limitation of the study.

As you prepare and conduct the project other considerations may arise. While not all of these can be predicted, by being prepared that something *may* crop up during your study will provide you with a greater readiness to respond quickly and effectively. Of course you should always head into a project with confidence that all will run smoothly, but you should also be prepared.

Over to you . . .

At this stage it would be worthwhile to consider the following questions that concern the consent process. They are discussed in detail later, but we ask you to note your initial thoughts here.

- How will you go about gaining informed consent from a four-year-old child?

- How will you know if the child fully understands the nature of the research proposed?

- How will you validate that the consent given by the child is in fact what the child wants?

How will researching with these children intentionally inform your study?

It is critical from an ethical perspective that you are sure that researching with children is absolutely necessary. Some projects can be conducted by accessing readily available data from other studies. The process of including children in research may be time-consuming, costly and an intrusion into the lives of many people, not least the children themselves. Children should not be included in research for entertainment or amusement purposes or to simply confirm an already well-known premise. If they are to be included, both you and the children should be clear in the understanding that their involvement is very important to the outcomes of the study (Harcourt and Sargeant 2011). If in doubt, leave them out.

Conceptualizing the project: including children's perspectives?

The sociology of childhood conceptualizes children as active and competent beings and key witnesses to their own lives (Mayall 2002). Each child can provide insights into our current understanding about children, how they mature, their processes of cognitive and emotional development, and their place in the world as influenced by their experienced and physical environments (Archard 2004; Prasad 2007). The sociology of childhood positions children as competent social actors in their own right and, as such, including them in the development of research is considered highly desirable.

Child voice, and children's perspectives more generally, are gaining increased attention within child-related professions and are being recognized as paramount at the grass roots level (Lundy 2007). Less recognized, however, is a broader societal acceptance of the capacities of modern children to personally deal with and process the information of their everyday lives (Sargeant 2010). While some researchers position each child as a competent and capable contributor to research endeavours, others view children as simply incapable of actively participating in the research preparation process.

Why consult children at the beginning?

The majority of research projects that involve children are not directly informed by the children's perspective. Projects that seek to develop programmes, services or treatments *for* children will necessarily involve children, perhaps in trials or experiments to determine any benefits. In these cases, the perspectives of the children regarding the actual project are not necessary. However, the children's active participation and consent to the research is usually essential. For this reason the perspectives of the children involved regarding the procedures used by the researcher should be considered during the project development.

Within any research endeavour, it is possible for children to assume a range of roles: co-participant, data generator, beneficiary, adviser, informant or subject. Of these, the most comprehensive role of children in a research project is that of the co-participant or co-researcher (Harcourt and Sargeant 2011).

While there is a growing emphasis on children as co-researchers (Smith *et al.* 2002), a difficulty with much (well-intentioned) research exists when children are included only *after* the topic has been identified (Moore *et al.* 2008). Researchers often act according to what they as adults consider being in the child's best interests, which may lead to ignoring children's own wishes and views (Valentine 1999). Similarly, Grover (2004: 91) states 'it is time that children are regarded as experts on their own subjective experience'. As we have previously suggested, traditional notions of defined and predetermined transitions through the human lifespan have positioned children as growing to *become* someone (e.g. a 7-year-old, adolescent, worker). This view of children considers that children cannot provide reliable information from the position of *being* a child. Attitudes of suspicion towards children's capacities are slowly diminishing as the weight of evidence that supports the capable/agentic child position continues to grow. When conceptualizing the project design consider and take appropriate steps, where possible, in order to provide children with a thoughtful level of agency at all stages of the research.

Ponder this . . .

Philip, an early years teacher and postgraduate university student, was considering an action research project that was to be based on his work in a preschool. He considered a number of issues that were interesting to him, mainly to do with curriculum. While the university he attended assumed that the action researcher alone would establish a topic and research question, Philip had been reading some interesting work by Alison Clark from the UK. He decided he would like to include the children in his centre in some way through a consultation group, but was not quite sure how to begin.

The most challenging aspect for researchers is around how to honour and facilitate participation by children. As discussed in Chapter 1, ideas of children and childhood are framed according to differing criteria. Contemporary views of children reflect the influence of the current social and economic dominant forces and will change again over time. When beginning a research project that relates to, or might include children, it is important to consider the key informants to your project. Traditional sources for the development of research projects include scholarly texts, literature reviews, previous studies, research methodology texts, expert consultation and collaborations with other researchers within and across disciplines. A developing contemporary approach also seeks to include children directly as consultants to the project development and in some cases as co-researcher or collaborators with equal status (Harcourt and Conroy 2005).

It is well acknowledged that children provide the 'missing perspectives of those who experience the effects of existing educational policies-in-practice' (Cook-Sather 2002: 3). Including children with authenticity in the research process represents a form of child advocacy, which then involves raising the status of children and increases their position as social agents. Children should be included in the endeavour as early as possible, beginning with the provision of full explanatory information.

Within contemporary child-related research there is an emerging acknowledgement of children's rights and agency, which in turn is acting as a provocation for inclusive research practice. However, as childhood is neither easily nor commonly defined, many studies relating to children are often predetermined by adults based on their assumptions of children and childhood. While such assumptions may be accurate, the risk of imperfect research mounts when all of the available views of childhood are not considered, particularly those held by the children themselves.

Over to you . . .

To what extent do your project preparations consider how children and their perspectives will be included over the entire research process?

Consulting children about the project

Including the views of other children who meet the same criteria as those targeted in your research project can provide critical insights into how the project, particularly the data collection, might be conducted. Many of the dilemmas that confront researchers during the data collection phase might be prevented or at least flagged if some children are consulted during the project's development.

Ponder this . . .

Renee, a university student, was preparing to conduct a research project that focused on children's experiences of physical education (PE). She thought it would be a good idea to make some observations in PE classes, conduct interviews with teachers and also ask the children some questions about their PE experiences. In developing the project Renee considered that she should consult with children to make sure she was asking appropriate questions. Even though the children she was planning to consult with would not be involved in the main study, she believed she needed formal ethical approval to approach the children for advice.

A growing body of recent research, which includes children's voice and participation in the research design process, offers some interesting insights into the opportunities and challenges of this inclusive approach. While these studies primarily disseminate results of the focused research as is appropriate in any research context, they also demonstrate the feasibility of such an approach. These published works provide exemplars of ethical methodological preparation, design and conduct that include children at all stages of the process. However, it is essential to note that consulting with children at the design and conceptualization phase requires thoughtful deliberation for a number of reasons.

- These children are not subjects of the research but are consultants to a project and therefore do not fall under the conditions of ethical clearance measures that protect researchers and participants within a main project. As such, you must seek the approval and consent of the design participants (and their guardians) in accordance with protocols, such as local privacy laws, to assure legal protection and appropriate conduct.

- In most cases it would not be advisable that the co-designers or consultants to a project also participate in the project as a perceived conflict of interest or bias may impact on the authenticity and reporting of the results.

- If a researcher, particularly a student researcher or one not in a child-specific field (e.g. law), has limited experience or expertise in consulting with children but remains committed to including children's perspective in the research design, it is advisable that another suitably skilled researcher should be recruited to guide these consultative discussions alongside the less experienced researcher.

Including children in the conceptualization phase of a research endeavour is not as straightforward as might be first thought. In addition, access to children, time constraints and the skills of the research team may prevent such full consultations from occurring at the design of the process.

An alternative approach, which can include children's perspectives on the project design and method, is to structure the project in such a way that includes pilot testing and revision. You may also consider modification of the design and/or refining the methods throughout the project. Such refinement within the project proper is usually only possible in a qualitative design, although it is important to reflect on the possible roles of the child consultant or child participant at each of the key stages of a research project.

In the hermeneutic context of research, it may be beneficial and necessary to describe the effects of the engagement of the children and the data analysis had on the researcher. While such a reflexive exercise is probably not at the core of your research or reflected in your research questions, it does provide an opportunity to put into play another perspective.

> **Over to you . . .**
>
> What will be the main role/s of the children in your project?

International treaties and local laws

It is important to consider international treaties such as the UNCRC and the associated General Comments, local laws that relate to children such as privacy, child protection and duty of care and, any departmental policies that govern research involving children in your particular context. Familiarization with these documents is important and should be considered early in the project's development. This will be particularly relevant if you are seeking to include children as consultants to the project in addition to participants at the data collection stage. It is also important to understand that there are a large number of protocols and approval processes that govern research involving children that can delay or jeopardize a project's progress. These logistical barriers can usually be overcome if addressed fully and thoughtfully at the planning stage. It is not advised that a project is simply developed in order the gain formal ethical approval, as this is likely to undermine the quality of the research, unsatisfactorily answer the research question/s and contribute very little to the knowledge base relating to children and childhood.

The UNCRC

Consider the non-negotiable mandates of the UNCRC (United Nations 1989) which all countries, with the exception of the USA, have ratified. The UNCRC has provided a significant platform from which to include children's views on issues that affect their lives. By ratifying the UNCRC, a country undertakes a legal, moral and ethical commitment to accord children their rights.

The UNCRC is widely regarded by the international community as the most comprehensive statement on children's rights. As such, it provides a foundation for developing policies and making decisions in all matters relating to children up to the age of 18 years. It resonates with the sociology of childhood and childhood studies where children are positioned as social and political actors, with the agency to actively participate in their society. In addition, the UNCRC clearly values children as capable and competent *beings* and therefore respects their ability to contribute valid opinions.

While the UNCRC consists of 54 Articles, our discussion focuses primarily on those related to children's right to participation as it relates to research.

Over to you . . .

If you have not already done so, familiarize yourself with the UNCRC at www.unicef.org/crc/

Children's right to be heard

Article 12.1 (children's right to a voice) of the convention is often cited when seeking to include children in research as it explicitly declares that children who are capable have the right to be heard. However, Article 12.1 also proves to be particularly problematic due to varying definitions and adult perspectives on the capacities of children, particularly younger children. It states in full that:

> States parties shall assure to the child who is capable of forming his or her own views the right to express those views freely in all matters affecting the child, the views of the child being given due weight in accordance with the age and maturity of the child.
>
> (United Nations 1989)

A direct outcome of enacting Article 12.1 in your research project rests with the effect on the children involved. Limber and Flekkoy (1995) suggest that when given opportunities to be heard in matters concerning them, young children develop feelings of self-esteem and competence, which, in turn, are contributors to democratic citizenship. This notion of the agentic child (Danby and Baker 1998), the competent social actor in their own right, is consistent with the concept of the child as a reliable informant in the research process.

When seeking to research with, on or about children, it is worth while to carefully reflect on the key intentions of Article 12.1 and consider your own interpretation based on your reflections about children and childhood completed in Chapter 1.

Over to you . . .

- What does Article 12.1 of the UNCRC mean to you?

- How will Article 12.1 impact your study?

Having reflected on Article 12.1 and more broadly in the context of the UNCRC, consider your research questions again and the methods you anticipate using for data collection. Your question may explicitly identify aspects relating to Article 12.1 such as:

- how children may conceptualize [your topic];
- what children's reported experiences may be around [your topic];
- what children's perspectives might be of [your topic];
- what children's opinions could be on [your topic];
- what children may have to say about [your topic];
- how children might express themselves through artefacts such as writing, photography, drawing, music and so on.

If your research question has the potential for seeking children's views and perspectives embedded into it, your task in developing an appropriate child-centred research design can be guided firmly by the research question itself. Your design therefore will focus on the methods suitable to elicit children's views on your specific topic. However, other research questions relating to children and childhood may not explicitly seek the child's perspective. Such questions might include wording such as:

- What are the effects of early intervention phonics training on literacy outcomes for early years students?
- How does shared parenting impact on children's participation in extra-curricula activity?
- What are the impacts of food advertising during children's television on children's fitness levels?

As we highlighted in a previous reflexive activity, while directly affecting children and likely to include children in the study in some way, these research questions do not have a specific focus on the perspectives of the children. Studies such as these are not exempt from the Articles of the UNCRC, although the consideration of children's participation in the research is not driven by the research question. Instead, the ethical inclusion and active participation of children in the study will have to be explicitly and embedded in the research design. In these cases, Article 12.1 should be applied throughout the research design in such a way that is *complementary* to the focus of the research.

Consider the extent to which your project will support the intentions of Article 12.1. Is this explicit in the wording of your research questions or can it be developed in a later discussion? Do your research questions plainly identify children's perspectives as an intended outcome of the study, or will the children's voice and active participation be facilitated through your research design?

Over to you . . .

To what extent do your research questions respond to Article 12.1 of the UNCRC?

Children's right to express

Having now reflected on Article 12.1, now consider Article 13 of the UNCRC. Article 13 extends the rights of children to have a voice by providing for the right to choose their mode of communication and to be free to seek and gather information. It states that:

> The child shall have the right to freedom of expression; this right shall include freedom to seek, receive and impart information and ideas of all kinds, regardless of frontiers, either orally, in writing or in print, in the form of art, or through any other media of the child's choice.

(United Nations 1989)

In previous centuries, children were expected to work and contribute to the wealth or survival of their community. Leisure activities were regarded with suspicion and even the invention and commercial development of toys was blamed for the corruption of children's minds; much like the Internet and computer games are today (Karasavidou 2004). Prior to the advent of the Internet, television was regarded and to a large extent remains as the medium that would most adversely affect children's lives (Levin 1998; Karasavidou 2004; Simpson 2004).

As with earlier times, community leaders, teachers and parents proclaim to have the interests of children at the forefront. They seek to protect children from the external influences that will adversely affect their growth. However, by introducing access barriers to the media, and the information available therein, children's rights to information are being withheld. This situation is often debated within the context of what is in the best interests of the child. However, it is also possible that those same groups who are seeking to protect children may in fact be encouraging them to secretly seek out censored media. If children actively seek out information sources without adult knowledge, because they are forbidden, the opportunity to teach critical reasoning provide moral guidance and the judicious use of these information sources is then denied.

Over to you . . .

How does your planned project consider the mandate offered by Article 13 of the UNCRC?

The implications of Article 13 are clear, but often ignored, within research activities. Many projects, when designed by adults, do not offer the participating children a choice of communication tools. Limiting the opportunities for children to communicate in their chosen way, be it verbal, written, digitally through photographs, through artwork or any other available means, will necessarily limit the richness of the data and also the number of available participants, particularly in early childhood research.

By making available a range of choices for the children, you are more likely to experience willing participants as their confidence in their own communication techniques is displayed. Will you prescribe the means by which children engage in your project or will they be offered a choice of communication? How will you make this decision (observation, etc.)? While such considerations are often complicated by logistics, planning for this in advance can greatly enhance the quality of your data. Again, the analysis of multiple forms of data may require extra training or skill development but such challenges offer you a unique learning opportunity.

Article 13 is also crucial when supporting children's right to access information relating to your research. All parents or stakeholders must provide approval and consent for you to conduct your research with children, seeking further information about your study when necessary. Children also have the right to be fully informed of the intent and nature of the project they are being asked to be involved in. Children should be free to seek further information about your work and from an inclusive standpoint; you should be prepared to respond respectfully to their requests. It is important to consider these issues at the planning stage so that you are better prepared for any contingency.

Privacy

When considering the context of your study you must ensure that all aspects and procedures in your project conform to all relevant privacy legislation. Privacy may be protected under a range of privacy, anti-discrimination or information laws, which may be different according to local authorities. Children's right to privacy is also protected under Article 16 of the UNCRC: 'No child shall be subjected to arbitrary or unlawful interference with his or her privacy, family, home or correspondence, nor to unlawful attacks on his or her honour and reputation' (United Nations 1989).

You should become familiar with the local laws to determine whether your research represents any breach of the various privacy principles and, if so, whether the public interest in the research substantially outweighs the public interest in respecting privacy, in which case a local and institutional authorization would be required.

Child protection

Child protection responsibilities take precedence when weighing up the merits and benefits of any research project. It is essential that you are familiar with any local child protection protocol and laws regarding disclosure by children of harm. Most jurisdictions have procedures in place to protect and safeguard children and young people involved in research. It is also likely that you will be required to undergo criminal history checks prior to working with any children.

Ethical dilemmas and issues around confidentiality, trust and the relationship between the researcher and research participant may arise and should be carefully considered, particularly if the confidentiality and trust of a child must be broken. It is important to explain to participants at the beginning of the research process that confidentiality will be breached if a concern or disclosure is made about the safety of a child.

Duty of care

Researchers have a responsibility to ensure that children and young people involved in research are able to access age appropriate support for any issues and concerns that may arise as a result of their participation. You also have a responsibility to be informed of any cultural, religious and other such differences among your intended research participants. In some circumstances you may have a responsibility to follow up after the project to ensure the child participants have received any necessary support.

Committing to the ethical and informed inclusion of children

The traditional ways of researching children and childhood through observation and formal testing protocols without the inclusion of children's perspectives are now increasingly considered to be outmoded. The emerging commitment to affording children their human rights and allowing them to exercise those rights in the same way other people do presents both challenges and opportunities for the research community. Bessant (2006) suggests that as the wider adult community better appreciates children's capacities, even in the very young, the tradition of speaking on behalf of children is no longer simple, straightforward or acceptable. While a developmental view of childhood is convenient when preparing a research project, it is significantly flawed and ironically does not reflect our increasing knowledge of children's capacities even at a very young age.

During your initial recruitment of children for your project, it is essential that they are not only empowered to opt in to your project but also that they are aware that they can also withdraw at any time. Bessant (2006) asserts that informed consent by the participant is essential and that the measure of explanation regarding withdrawal of consent needs full consideration so that children understand that their initial consent is not a one-off and final decision (Valentine 1999). These issues are discussed in further detail in Chapter 4.

Fisher (2005) notes that many children and young people do not always believe or fully understand that participation is voluntary. Their right to withdraw is often hampered by external experiences, expectations and/or pressure. Notions of expected compliance and rule-following behaviour impact such capacities. This is particularly evident with research conducted in the school context where the setting itself presents as a coercive element (Valentine 1999). In education settings, teachers often hold certain privileges and status that allows researchers to benefit from institutional norms about children's compliance (Valentine 1999). In these contexts an increased effort must be taken to ensure the children are clearly encouraged to question *anything* they feel is wrong. It is equally important that you take direct action to address children's concerns whether it is through further explanation or by modifying the procedures you are applying.

If you are successful in empowering the child participants to consider themselves competent informants to the process, it is possible that the children will hold an expectation that any issues raised by them will be directly acted upon. It is essential that the full intent, objectives, benefits and limitations of the research in the context of how your participants will be affected should be clearly explained to the children. The allocation of authority is so infrequently afforded to children and as such, misunderstood expectations can lead to disenchantment with adults if the children do not experience any direct personal outcomes of the research.

Recognition of children as a distinct social group involves acknowledgement of their experiential knowledge. Mayall's (2002) research in Britain found that children in school settings identified themselves as in a subordinate position to adults (teachers and parents) reinforcing an imbalance between their own and adults' social standing. Neale (2004: 98) suggested that 'we often act as if children are not there' which renders children to a position as passive recipients. If researchers are to provide valid contribution to the knowledge base on children and childhood, recognition must be given to the child's standpoint.

Researchers should address the extent to which they consider young children as capable citizens with recognition to the benefits of society as a whole. Kulynych (2001) noted that younger children are not seen as reliable reporters even of their own experience, and as such we rarely ask them for their own perspective (Thomas and Campling 2000). Children may be more knowledgeable of the adult world than in previous years (Smith and Wilson 2002), but adults cannot profess a reciprocal knowledge of children's perspectives (Sargeant 2010). By focusing on the child as an agent, a social actor who participates in constructing knowledge through their daily experiences we can apply a more strategic inclusion of children's knowledge in our research endeavours.

Limber and Flekkoy (1995) suggest that when given opportunities to be heard in matters concerning them, young children develop feelings of self-esteem and competence, which, in turn, are contributors to citizenship in a democracy. This notion of the agentic child (Danby and Baker 1998), the competent social actor in their own right, is consistent with the notion of the child as a reliable informant in the research process.

The process of personal authority is a key area of concern when working with children. Children's capacities to assert their views and express autonomy are contextual and relational rather than developmental. Denying this autonomy is only legally valid when considered in the best interests of the child (Valentine 1999). However, if we concur with the image of children as capable and competent, children who appropriate and reproduce aspects of their culture through interactions with others (Corsaro 1997), then restricting their wishes and freedoms is likely to be against their best interests. Agentic children possess the capabilities and competences to meet new challenges with curiosity and motivation (Woodrow 2001) and should be afforded the opportunities to practise these skills whenever possible.

Ponder this . . .

Charlotte realized her project idea was potentially in breach of the UNCRC. Her focus was on children's ability to adapt to different teaching methods within her Grade 4 classroom. Her data collection plans included teacher observations and a survey of the parents' and her colleagues' opinions of the different activities that were being trialled. She would also hand out a questionnaire in class time for the children to complete, with a space for their name included. The results would then inform changes to her curriculum and pedagogy.

As seen in Charlotte's story above, the implications of the UNCRC are apparent in even the most simple of projects. To address Charlotte's concerns, some relatively minor adaptations to the data collection process can address her potential concerns. Such adaptations might include:

- Offering the children a choice of how to respond to the questionnaire either by online or handwritten form, by drawing picture responses or by conducting short interviews using the same questions.
- Offering the children the option to complete the questionnaire anonymously or in an interview with another less familiar adult.
- Ensuring that no formal testing would occur during the research period so that the children were not disadvantaged by possible adverse results in the school records.
- Offer the children the opportunity to review her analysis at key stages of the project to ensure she was representing their views appropriately.
- Engage the children in the change process, so that they have a voice in any changes to the curriculum and teaching and learning practice.

As you can see, sometimes it is relatively simple refinement that can bring a project in line with the UNCRC mandates. The next section of this chapter shifts in focus to establishing and maintaining positive interactions between you and the children in your study. Particular attention is paid to interpersonal relationships, power dynamics and some of the key barriers to successful engagement with your participants.

The researcher–participant relationship

It might be a worthwhile activity to simply jot down all of the possible effects your project could have on your participants, and then rank them from least likely to most likely to occur. The list you create could be quite long – and even the most unlikely items should not be ruled out as impossible. In research involving children, anything can happen. One of the areas you have most control over is your role in building a positive working relationship with your participants. Critical to the success of almost all research projects is an effective professional relationship between the researcher and the participants. In research involving children, the importance of this relationship is multiplied.

Including children at all stages of the research process is considered to contribute to establishing rapport and trust thereby breaking down some of the imbalances due to age and power. Ultimately, however, the degree to which children are included as co-researchers remains at the discretion of the adult. The 'concept of the homogenised powerful competent adult, remains dominant within discourses on doing research with children' (Thomson 2007: 212). The full inclusion of children as co-researchers remains a rarity in research, not for reasons of the child's competence or capacity but mainly because of their marginalization and adult perceptions. When children are included, usually during the data collection stage, the balance of power often remains firmly with the researcher, who may be oblivious to the effect this is having on the children involved.

In participatory research, there is no substitute for respect and empathy with participants. Grover (2004) noted the importance of establishing trusting relationships to overcome the predisposition of children to present what they believe they are supposed to say in a research context. The context – school, home or another setting where children gather – in which research is undertaken can shape the ethical implications of working with children. The formal structures of compliance, privacy and confidentiality can all reinforce an already uneven power distribution in the research relationship. The relationship between you (as the researcher) and the children (as your participants) requires careful consideration prior to and during your interactions, especially in relation to notions of power.

The balance of power between you and your participants

Building a professional rapport as discussed above can be a significant influence on the success of your work. Regardless of the efforts you take to make the children comfortable with you and the project, it is an inescapable fact that a power imbalance will endure throughout the project. By virtue of the fact that you are an adult with external and local authorization to study the lives of children, you hold a delicate and privileged position as a researcher. In addition, a number of other influences on the power relationship between you and the children may be present. Some can be overcome or reduced with careful planning and communication, while others are simply unavoidable. Here are some examples.

The teacher–researcher

The dual roles of the teacher–researcher can sometimes resemble a Jekyll and Hyde situation. As a teacher you have a duty of care, are responsible for the children's daily routines, educational programme, behaviour and social development among other things. As a researcher you have a much narrower focus that is determined by the parameters of your project. How you balance these roles is important for the authenticity of the project, as well as the continued educational development of the children as your students. It is very important that you understand these roles, when they overlap and where they diverge. It is equally important that the children understand this complex situation so they can negotiate their own roles as either student or research participant. Depending on your study, normal behavioural expectations of the students might be suspended during the mode of specific research activities, or they may be assumed to continue. Either way, the students must be made aware of this, otherwise your usual role as teacher and authority figure will be expected and with that all of the power that resides with a teacher will be maintained. This might be okay and may not affect the study, but if it does, you may need to reconsider how your research is continued.

The stranger–researcher

If your research brings you into contact with children who you have not met before, you may well need to spend some time getting to know them and letting them get to know you. This time can be spent establishing a professional but friendly relationship with the children that should also include the establishment of your ground rules or expectations for their participation. One advantage the teacher–researcher has over the stranger–researcher is the pre-existing relationship and authority that is present. As a stranger–researcher you should not assume the children will be readily willing or able to comply with your instructions that relate to the project, or that their behaviour in general will be positive. In most cases, with a full explanation of the process, the children will be willing to help you with your project as long as they are confident and interested in what you are seeking to achieve.

As with any activity, if your interactions are disturbing, confusing or boring to the children, their willingness to continue will diminish. Time management, appropriate communication, patience and an awareness of your own and the children's moods will promote a smooth process. Your own competence with the children can influence their behaviours and as such it is important, particularly in relation to safety issues, that they understand which instructions are non-negotiable and which are optional. It is also worth while prior to meeting the children to note down what your expectations will be and how you will ensure the children understand them.

Over to you . . .

- Will you have sole responsibility for the children's safety and well-being during the study?

- How will you ensure the children's behaviour remains safe?

- Will the children understand which of your instructions are non-negotiable?

- How will you communicate these instructions?

- Are there any consequences for non-compliance?

Children's capacities

Aside from the age difference between the researcher and the children, a number of other key influences require attention when considering children's willingness and capacity to engage in your research. The physical, emotional, cognitive, psychological and social capacities of each child will differ based on a range of factors. Each of these can impact directly on the power relationship between you and your participants. Some of the key issues relating to these elements are discussed below.

Physical

Probably the most obvious representation of the power imbalance between children and researchers is physical size. Naturally, in most cases, you are going to be physically bigger than the children (with the possible exception of research involving adolescents). The physical differences between the researcher and child can have a number of effects. Initially the children may feel intimidated or fearful of your close presence, which can cause a defensive reaction where the child may physically withdraw. Other considerations of physical aspects include beards or glasses with very young children, tattoos and/or piercings, unusual hair colour or style, physical disabilities or challenges, and other physical attributes that may cause children to feel uncomfortable or intimidated. You may need to reconsider how you present as an adult prior to meeting the children.

Emotional

Traditionally the tumultuous transition period between childhood and adulthood has been considered normal adolescent development. While the majority of young people make the transition from adolescence to adulthood without major troubles, a significant number of adolescents do experience mental health problems (Sawyer *et al.* 2001). When making judgements about someone else's emotional state, we have to be very careful to recognize that our perceptions are just that – they belong to us. When we 'assess' we do so from the perspective of our knowledge, beliefs and cultural biases. These are informed by our own experiences that may not align with the children's.

The moods and emotions of younger children are sometimes harder to recognize and even harder to predict. These considerations are most apparent when the research focuses on sensitive topics that may cause an unintended and even more unexpected reaction. At all times, try to be ready for the unpredictable and have in place a strategy for the safe support of a child who experiences distress.

Cognitive

The cognitive capacity of your research participants should be considered in terms of the language and methods you select to apply in your study. It is important that the language you use to communicate with your participants is appropriate to their literacy levels. The ability to concentrate for long periods can also be influenced by a

Ponder this . . .

Andrew was trialling some new tablet technology in his class with a view to evaluate middle school children's ability to conduct independent research using the Internet. The students were being guided through the various ways to conduct research using search engines and sourcing news websites. One of the students 'surfed' to a news front page where the lead story detailed a recent car accident that had fatalities. The student read the headline then burst into tears and ran from the classroom.

Another student informed Andrew that the distressed student's family members had recently been critically injured in a car accident. Andrew thanked the student for the information and redirected the class back to the task. However, the whole class was now focused on the upset student and did not want to continue. Andrew knew this session was an important one that had taken weeks to schedule so he continued to press the students to resume the activity.

person's cognitive abilities and it is worth bearing in mind that children's brains tire as much as any other part of their body.

Psychological

Psychologically, humans are vulnerable to stress and as social beings are also vulnerable to illness when stress is chronic and social conditions are contributing to these high levels of stress. Some communities are more vulnerable than others because of a range of social conditions, the availability of resources or limited access to resources.

A number of 'at risk' groups and communities have been identified as being more vulnerable to developing mental health problems and/or illnesses. These include:

- victims of bullying;
- indigenous peoples;
- people living in rural and remote communities;
- people who abuse alcohol and other drugs;
- same sex attracted young people;
- children and young people who have experienced abuse;
- people with disabilities;
- children who are asylum seekers or refugees.

Although the above factors may need consideration, for a range of reasons, it is very important not to stereotype groups on the basis of certain characteristics or indicators of risk. For example, not all refugee children are at risk in terms of social-emotional well-being. But if you take the conditions that many asylum seekers live in as a result of ongoing disadvantage in a society, then risk factors begin to stack up against the community and hence against individuals.

Social

Social skills are generally described as the ability to facilitate positive interactions with other individuals and groups. While many social skills are learned through normal development, some individuals have social skill deficits that negatively affect their behaviour and seriously compromise their ability to interact effectively.

People do not behave in a vacuum. The social context powerfully prompts, maintains and provides natural consequences for all of us. It is clear that certain groups of people are more at risk of developing social and emotional problems as a result of circumstances that are often beyond their control. Young children, those with disabilities and the aged are especially vulnerable to abuse, exploitation and neglect because of their developmental profiles. They can be powerless in the face of abuse by those in authority, as well as those who are predisposed to being cruel or perpetrating abuse. As a key adult in these children's lives, even if only for a short time, it is important that you are aware of the potential risks that your involvement may provoke through no deliberate act on your behalf.

Summary

This chapter has focused on:

- an exploration of the dominant and recurring predicaments that researchers experience;
- the conceptualization of the research project and the roles of children;
- the importance of an inclusive focus on research with children that values children's perspectives;
- reasoning for consulting with children at the beginning of the project;
- the importance of familiarization with international treaties and local laws with a particular focus on the UNCRC;
- exploring the ethical dilemmas present as a result of the researcher–participant relationship;
- considering the balance of power between you and your participants;
- identified the key attributes of children and their potential impact on their participation.

3
Building a research team: the Researcher Capacity Analysis

Introduction

The research process can be either hindered or enhanced by the key abilities and competences of the research team recruited or available for a project. The bureaucratic obstacles of time, data, cost, training, blurring of research objectives, process of consent, ethics, motivation of participants, location and methods of data collection present increasing restrictions on the nature of the quantity (and quality) of research being conducted with children (Mahon *et al.* 1996; Smith *et al.* 2002). Bessant (2006) notes that because of ethical constraints and administrative issues, some researchers simply decide not to use methodologies that engage children in any way. This encourages and perpetuates a level of knowledge about children that does not directly seek or include their accounts. We consider this approach as not only *unethical* but *unnecessary* if an appropriate level of planning is undertaken prior to any project's commencement. Understanding the capacity of you and your team is critical to achieving this goal.

The Researcher Capacity Analysis (RCA) of the proposed research project should include considerations of methodology knowledge, breadth of interest, knowledge of ethics, experience with children and child-centred research tools. Some of the factors that impact on a researcher's capacity to complete a project may not be immediately obvious or predicted at the project conceptualization or design stage. Identification of these issues may not emerge until much later in the project but will still require resolution. As such, it is important to revisit the RCA a number of times to ensure the ongoing integrity of the project.

The RCA is organized around five key elements: Skills, Qualifications, Experience, Roles and Training. The first three elements, Skills, Qualifications and Experience, are representative of the attributes each member of the research team brings with them to the project as key contributors to a successful outcome. The final two elements represent how these will be 'put into play' in the context of the project. The roles and responsibilities of all participants, including the research participants, will need to be considered in relation to any additional training requirements that each participant may need in order to complete their research-related tasks.

Ponder this . . .

Rachel, a graduate sociology student, is interested in studying young children's anxiety when beginning primary school. Rachel has had three years' experience as a childcare assistant prior to going to university but has received no formal training in child development and learning.

Andrew is considering a Ph.D. and is proposing a pilot study that looks at children's anxiety during a visit to the dentist. Andrew is a dentist by profession and his research interest had stemmed from his personal experiences with some child patients. In his Masters degree he focused on parental coping mechanisms with their children's stress while undergoing dental treatment.

Carmel has been teaching in a university for nine years in the area of literacy. She is concerned that the Australian NAPLAN test, which tests children's literacy in Years 3, 5, 7 and 9 is causing high levels of anxiety in students, particularly the younger ones. She has been involved in a number of research projects involving children in the past.

While the contexts of their respective interests are quite different, Carmel, Rachel and Andrew share an interest in children's anxiety during a stressful event. They would like to submit a joint research grant application and are currently evaluating their joint and individual strengths.

Considering these attributes at each stage of the project from development to dissemination increases the likelihood of ethical and authentic research with children. A well-considered RCA will embed ethical decision-making and practices at all stages of the research endeavour. The RCA can also assist you to understand both the strengths and weaknesses of your research team, even if this is a team of one. For student researchers the RCA is particularly important. You will be better prepared if you can identify in advance when you are likely to need the assistance of others, usually your supervisor but also other experts in the field, to successfully complete your project. The main elements that should be considered in an RCA are described below.

Skills

The successful conduct of a research project is dependent on the skills that researchers have that are relevant to the project design. Many studies with children include observations, interviewing, group activities and direct instruction. While these interactions might be seen as low risk, they do require particular skills to achieve the research task and preserve the psychological and emotional integrity of the child participants.

Research projects that are examining sensitive topics related to the emotional well-being of children and young people may involve the area of psychology or counselling which are, of course, specialized skills.

Some interviews; for example, those relating to research in the legal sphere, also require specialist subject knowledge and the skilled translation of this knowledge into a language appropriate to the age, maturity and capacity of the child.

Medical research with children will certainly require a high level of procedural skill, particularly if the task involves invasive methods such as the administration of medication, taking blood samples or other medical procedures.

However, we would suggest that one of the key skills needed in any research that includes children requires that the researcher/s have the ability to communicate effectively with children regardless of age. This is a significant skill, one that takes time and practice to master. If the researcher is coming from a field other than those that have regular and sustained interactions with children, such as teaching, it may be an area in which they will need to access further professional development. It would be most unwise to embark on a project without someone on the team who is very experienced in this area.

Qualifications

Many of the procedures that require a high level of skill such as those in medical research usually require a formal level of qualification before they can be carried out. The application of formal psychological testing will also require specific certification. For student researchers these responsibilities and duty of care will usually fall to your supervisors and the conduct of medical or formal counselling of children can only occur under strict supervision. For legal and ethical reasons these qualifications are essential elements to the make up of your research team.

Other methods of data collection such as informal interviews may not require supervision but the overall level of qualification of the researcher can affect the procedures and quality of the project. While not the sole determinant of a successful research outcome, it is more likely that higher levels of education and in particular research training will enhance the project's success. It is important to at least consider if the research team members have qualifications formally recognizing their skills. The range of qualifications you have might not necessarily relate to research with children but in some other ways they can be useful in informing your practice.

Experience

A critical factor in researching with children is the level of experience your team has, not only in conducting research either with or without children but also with children in general. As discussed in Chapter 1, developing a research project that involves children offers many unique considerations. For those planning to research with children from fields where regular contact with children can be rare such as non-paediatric healthcare, business or law, the considerations are multiplied. By identifying the nature and level of experience each of the research team members bring to the project, you can identify where your strengths are and what type of project your team is best suited to conduct. A research team, for example, with very little experience with young children would be best advised to seek guidance before conducting any work with this group. In the same way, many of the specific behaviours of children with disabilities need careful consideration and expertise when interacting.

However, experience with children alone does not guarantee a project's success. Being aware of your conceptualizations of children and childhood, a well-established set of procedures and your ability to remain objective and professional during all interactions with your participants are essential in any project.

Roles

Depending on the size of your research team, members will be expected to assume specific or even multiple roles based on their skills, qualifications and experience. The requirements of the project itself will also present a number of demands on the research team. These roles should be clearly identified and designated early in the project development so that effective planning can take place. Any weaknesses or gaps in the team's capacity to complete the study can be identified. If these roles are identified and allocated early the project can either be adapted to suit the team's capacities or the team can be bolstered or upskilled where required without disruption to the project during the main data collection and analysis phases. At this point, not only are the roles of the research team members important to designate but also you should understand your specific expectations of the children and their participation. This early consideration is important, particularly if the children will be given the opportunity to provide input into the project design. Some of the key roles in most research projects include: principal or chief investigator, literature reviewer, interviewer, observer, participant, analyst (statistical), analyst (text, qualitative), technical adviser, supervisor, report writer and/or disseminator.

Training

Having considered the skills, qualification, experience and roles of the research team, the RCA can then be completed by focusing on the required training each member might need to fulfil their obligations to the project. Such training might relate to the data collection procedures such as interviewing or observing, while other training might be centred on data analysis such as using statistical software, or qualitative data management tools. The extent to which training is required should be apparent, based on the completion of the other sections of the RCA.

When researching with children a particular challenge often centres on the researcher's capacity to effectively communicate with children, particularly younger children. These skills are often developed over time and specific training in this area is often difficult to access. Effective communication with the child participants can have a significant impact on the richness of the data and can sometimes 'make or break' a project. If after completing the RCA, skills and experience remain significantly deficient, some form of training is highly recommended or you might have to seriously reconsider the viability of conducting the research.

It is important to consider in the context of the role designations, that the children may themselves need some guidance and training in the research process. Whether the children act as co-researchers or as subjects of the research, their experience in contributing to a research project may in most cases be limited. Of particular importance are their perspectives on the power dynamic between the adult researcher and themselves. As discussed in other sections, the process of recruitment and establishing a positive working relationship with the children may take some time and should be considered as part of the research training process.

The RCA in action

As an audit tool, the RCA can be applied in two ways. The RCA can be applied to analyse each participant according to the attributes they hold (and need) to fully participate in the project. The examples presented below demonstrate how the RCA can be applied to evaluate the capacity of each team member to contribute to the project. In addition, the RCA can be applied in order to analyse the project requirements in terms of what is required of the whole team to complete the study. In this exercise the names of the participants are applied to the required capacities so that any missing elements/team-member skills can be identified.

Tables 3.1 and 3.2 provides examples of the RCA template for the RCA process that constitutes a pre-research audit of the researcher team members and research-team's capacity to develop and conduct the project. Appendix 2 (see p. 100) provides a complete template for your use. The first template allows you to identify each team member's attributes and possible contributions to the project. Column 2 of the RCA allows you to identify the current strengths and supportive factors that will enable the project's success and nominate in column 3 your current capacity to meet these needs.

The second template enables the evaluation of the overall project requirements and provides an opportunity to allocate responsibility or recognition to the key members of the team according to the identified attributes. The RCA allows you to identify areas for development or enhancement that may threaten the success of the project and provide a description of the intended or needed response so that these deficits in the project design are addressed.

Table 3.1 Researcher Capacity Analysis: individual

Researcher attributes		
Team member name:		
Attribute/s		Available/ required?
Skills		
Qualifications		
Experience		
Roles		
Training		

Table 3.2 Researcher Capacity Analysis: project

Project attributes			
Project title:			
Attribute/s		Available/ required?	Team member
Skills			
Qualifications			
Experience			
Roles			
Training			

Over to you . . .

Having completed a detailed self-assessment of the project team through the RCA, two key questions remain:

1 What research team attributes will ensure the success of the project?
2 What research team attributes are still required for the success of the project?

Before progressing any further you should give careful consideration to these questions and develop a plan for how you will address these needs.

Summary

This chapter has focused on:

- The interplay between the skills, experience and qualifications of the research team members.
- A framework for developing and assessing the competence of the research team through the RCA.
- The importance of the research team's focus on its own capacity to conduct a quality and ethically sound project.

Phase 1 checklist

As you prepare to begin the design of the project, take a few minutes to gather your thoughts on the discussions presented in Phase 1. Consider what areas you are now more comfortable with and those ideas you need to develop further. The following checklist may assist in guiding your deliberations.

Task	Complete Yes/No/In progress
✓ Developed a detailed communication strategy for when you will meet with the children	
✓ Considered the impact of the research on the children involved	
✓ Considered seeking advice directly from children about your planned project	

Task	Complete Yes/No/In progress
✓ Identified the extent and duration of the children's involvement in your project	
✓ Considered the key characteristics of your participants	
✓ Considered the context of the study	
✓ Familiarized with local and international laws relevant to your project, UNCRC, Privacy, Duty of care, etc.	
✓ Considered your role and possible influence on the participants	
✓ Considered the expected capacities of the children you will invite to participate	
✓ Conducted an RCA and addressed any deficits present in your research team	

By this stage, you should have a clear idea of *how* and *why* your project will contribute to the knowledge base on childhood and how you expect children to be *included* in the research process. You will have also identified the strengths and weaknesses of your research team, or if you are a solo researcher, your own capacity to successfully complete your project. You are now ready to move on to the next chapter, which will discuss the beginnings of Phase 2 of the research process: the research design. It will address the implementation and organization of the project proper.

4

Phase 2 – research design

Introduction

Each project will necessarily adopt a particular research method that reflects the key aims of the overall research question. These approaches extend along a continuum from complete detachment from the children (objectivity) to a more fully immersed engagement in terms of the participation of children. Having fortified your conceptualizations in Phase 1 and identified a philosophical alignment with a particular research methodology and established a clear research question, your attention now turns to the research design. With the choice of method also come a number of ethical considerations that are unique to that approach.

> **Over to you . . .**
>
> Recap: What is your theoretical standpoint on children and childhood?

The role of children in the research

As we have suggested, within any research endeavour, children may assume a range of roles: co-researcher, participant, beneficiary, adviser or subject. Of these, the most authentic role of children in a research project is that of the co-researcher or equal participant. The project design should consider, and take appropriate steps where possible, to provide children with a thoughtful level of agency at all stages of the research. The most challenging aspect for governments, service providers, researchers and practitioners alike, has been how to honour and facilitate participation by children that is both authentic and ethical (Mason and Fattore 2005).

Over to you . . .

What active role or roles do you expect the children to have in your study?

The issues relating to research with children are often relevant to all research contexts (Mahon *et al.* 1996). Designing the research process to include children as active research participants and collaborators recognizes the inherent competence that children can offer. Children can transform and elaborate upon their experiences, through intentional symbolic representation of their experiences, and allow researchers to generate ideas and construct theories with them. Many qualitative studies reflect the more spectacular and visible aspects of children's attitudes and behaviour . . . conventionally 'normal' children are often considered as less interesting research subjects. This is a flawed assumption that can lead to an imbalance in the research relating to childhood where only the marginalized are studied.

Research design

The process of designing a project can be time-consuming and complicated depending on the focus of the research. While primarily concerned with seeking the most appropriate methods to answer the research question, it is essential to this process that a strong awareness of the welfare of the participants throughout the proposed project is maintained. As such, many of the issues identified and discussed in detail in 'Phase 3: conducting the research' require consideration at the design phase of the process. However, it is important that these same issues be reconsidered once the project is 'up and running'. This is relevant so that the original design can be verified for its ethical merit as well as its ability to answer the research question. It is often the case that many insights into the dilemmas of conducting research do not emerge until the project is well under way. Some of these dilemmas are discussed in Phase 3. Here, Phase 2 focuses on the elements of research design that are easily predicted but no less important in terms of ethical practice. These are the elements an authorizing body, such as a university ethics committee, may be interested in.

Social research represents a scientific technique that comprises the organized accumulation of methods to acquire knowledge. It is objective and can tell you things you do not expect. Like science, it consists of theory and observation but because it involves the study of people, social sciences are sometimes referred to as the soft sciences because their subject matter is fluid and hard to measure accurately. In empirical research (facts are assumed to exist prior to the theories that explain them) and the scientific manner in which theories are formed or tested produces objective results whereas the social sciences make an important contribution to our understandings of a wide variety of social issues.

Research approaches

The most common way that research designs are categorized is by distinguishing between quantitative and qualitative research. In its simplest form, quantitative research is concerned with numbers while qualitative research is concerned with words. Educational research was initially dominated by quantitative research designs because this was believed to be the superior form for gaining knowledge. Dissatisfaction with this approach has developed because the kinds of question that are relevant in naturalistic settings are not adequately answered by quantitative means. Mixed methods is an emerging and popular approach that draws from both qualitative and quantitative methods.

Quantitative research is characterized by a positivistic view that assumes science can explain the world in terms of what causes the things and the events that we observe. The key approaches used in quantitative studies include survey methods, and experimental design. Qualitative research is more likely to be personally intrusive than quantitative and as such makes it more vulnerable to ethical dilemmas. Qualitative research is characterized by some key approaches when researching with children including phenomenology, ethnographic research and participant observation, descriptive survey research, action research and case study. The following section discusses some of the key considerations when using these methods.

Phenomenological studies

Phenomenology represents a philosophical position where people are viewed as not things but actors; that is, they think and reflect on what they do. In phenomenological research, the focus is on the sense people make of the world rather than what the world appears to be. Phenomenology is intended to represent experiences through the lens of the participant.

In phenomenological studies the researcher must commence the study with an open mind and release themselves of preconceived opinions. A phenomenologist relies to a great extent on interviewing rather than observation with long, in-depth interviews, discussions and interactions a key characteristic. Because of the detail and descriptive data that is produced, the use of video and audio recording devices is more common.

The aim of phenomenology is to arrive at an understanding of the experience through the consciousness of the participants. Phenomenologists do not assume they know what events mean to the people they are examining, but seek meaning through the participants' direct account. Phenomenologists consider that the many ways of interpreting experiences are available through interacting with others and that reality, consequently, is socially constructed. Philosophies such as phenomenology and other qualitative research methods are capable of interpreting multiple realities and help us to better understand the human experience.

Ethnographic research

An ethnography constitutes a systematic, detailed way of studying a particular culture or social group, and *looks into* the meanings and values that group depicts. The term ethnography is often used interchangeably with participant observation. As a research method, ethnography is sometimes regarded as the product of a blend of methodologies, usually qualitative, that share the assumption that personal engagement with the subject is the key to understanding a particular culture or social setting.

Ethnography in its most characteristic form involves the ethnographer or participant observer, participating overtly or covertly, in people's daily lives for an extended period of time. Ethnographers watch what happens, listen to what is said, ask questions and collect whatever data are available to expose the issues that are the focus of research. The eventual written product – an ethnographic account – draws its data primarily from this fieldwork experience and usually emphasizes the descriptive detail. The researcher seeks to extrapolate meaning from observations and interactions with participants. In ethnographic studies the research question is usually formulated as a general statement, which may change according to what the researcher is observing and learning about the group they are observing.

Ethnographers spend a considerable amount of time collecting data by observing participants in their natural setting; for example, a study about the effects of certain teaching techniques on secondary school children. An ethnographer may also spend a lot of time as a participant observer in order to gain the most accurate perception of what is actually occurring.

Participant observation

Cohen *et al.* (2007) discuss how participant observers engage in the very activities they set out to observe. Participant observation is often applied by researchers who are working within a specific context of interest.

In covert participant observation, often the 'cover' is so complete that as far as the other participants are concerned, they are simply one of the group (Cohen *et al.* 2007). Covert participant observation presents some important ethical considerations when researching with children because the role of researcher and other key adults, such as the child's teacher, can sometimes be blurred. It is questionable whether such a method of deception should be considered at all. When submitting such a project for approval by gatekeepers a very strong case would need to be constructed.

Even when the children know the role of the participant observer, the power, supervisory and duty of care expectations on teachers may create some confusion for the children. They may have to interact with an adult who assumes multiple roles. Many practitioners have to negotiate an observer role but also periodically take on the position of key agent in order to effect change. There is a significant challenge in combining participation and observation so as to become capable of understanding the programme, as an insider, while describing the programme for outsiders. It is also important to consider the dual roles the child must also play in these situations. The children must negotiate the time they are solely a student and when they are participants in the research.

Descriptive research

Descriptive research, often called descriptive survey research, may be used most effectively within natural settings because these research experiences cannot be as realistically controlled as laboratory experiments. In contrast to laboratory experiences, descriptive research is valuable because it allows for the human element of research. Depending on the research question to be addressed, the methods of data collection usually involve surveys, interviews, observations and portfolios or a combination of these. Descriptive research involves collecting data in order to test hypotheses or to answer questions about the opinions of people about some topic or issue.

Action research

Action research can be described as a collaborative research methodology of self-reflective enquiry, which pursues rationality, and the understanding of social or educational practice (Kemmis 1988). It does this by using a cyclic or spiral process, which alternates between action and critical reflection, continuously refining methods, data and interpretation. A more comprehensive understanding of what happens in a social or education system takes shape as reflexivity is used. In practice-based action research, the role of the researcher is not that of an expert who *does* research, but that of a key stakeholder with a vested interest in the project outcomes. The action researcher acts as a catalyst in defining their problems clearly as they work towards effective solutions to the issues that concern them (Stringer 1996).

When researching with children it should be acknowledged that observers are always a factor in the research, no matter how neutral their position might be. This influence on the group must be recognized during an analysis or implementation activity in consideration of a possible 'Hawthorne Effect' where participants behave in a certain way, usually in support of the research, simply because they are being studied. The Hawthorne Effect was a catalyst for the development of action research as a methodology that assumes that understanding of situations and change occur simultaneously.

A number of considerations are important here. It is often the leader or the practitioner who regularly works with children who seek positive outcomes. The extent to which children are included in the process may vary. Children may not be only the subject of the research and informants to the success of the project as co-researchers. These blurred roles can affect the process of consent as the children balance their roles as participant and student. Children may think they are participating in normal class activities but because this classroom also doubles as a research context, the children should be provided with opportunities to consent to their contributions being used for research purposes. As with any research endeavour, researchers should provide opportunities for the children to withdraw from/opt out of the project at any time. However, in the context of practitioner research that is group-focused, offering individual children the choice to opt out is a significant challenge for the researcher as it may jeopardize the entire project. These issues are discussed in detail later.

Case study

A case study is an exploration of a bounded system, over time through detailed, in-depth data collection involving multiple sources of information rich in context. The context is bounded by time and place, and the case being studied usually comprises a programme, an event, an activity, a group or individuals. As Cohen *et al.* (2007) suggest, case study methodology enables us to relate more effectively to the environment, to recognize purpose, and to resolve conflicts. In qualitative research, the conclusions drawn from a particular study are tested or applied in specific settings with the aim of improving practice and educational outcomes. Often applied within the case study framework is the ethnographic approach of participant observation.

Development of data collection tools

When developing data collection tools appropriate for children, it is critical to consider all of the possible effects of your project on participants. However, some issues do not become apparent until the project is under way. If possible, a pilot study provides an opportunity to assess the appropriateness of your chosen method. It is also useful in gaining a clearer understanding of your own skills to apply the chosen methods.

Ponder this . . .

James was conducting a pilot study in a small metropolitan school with children aged 6 to 13. His intention was to seek the views of the children about the quality of teaching across all school levels by asking the same questions to all of the children. The older students were given a questionnaire to complete under the supervision of their class teachers (an ethical minefield, given the topic). The youngest of the students (those aged six and seven) and those who experienced reading and writing difficulties, were interviewed by James personally during class time. These students were asked exactly the same questions as those who were completing the written questionnaires. Their responses were recorded verbatim. Upon completion of the pilot study, James concluded that, while all of the children clearly understood the questions, the younger children experienced a level of intimidation when being interviewed and attempted to answer the questions to please him. A number of these children repeatedly asked James if they had answered correctly and despite reassurance from James they still appeared nervous during the process. James realized the unintended pressure his presence placed on the children and wondered out of respect for the children, should he not include this age group in the main study and focus on collecting only written responses.

The experience of James (above) not only revealed some of the considerations of the researcher being a stranger to the children and the potential power imbalances but also demonstrates the challenges in selecting appropriate research methods for the study. During the development of the study, James' main focus was on the questions and their validity in terms of the research question. Until he had completed the pilot study, the potential impact of his, and the teacher's presence on the participants had not been fully realized.

By directly interviewing the younger children, the researcher was unwittingly engaging two different research methods. An interview, regardless of its fine structure, has inherently different features, such as familiarity with the interviewer that could lead to a possible social desirability bias (Ary *et al.* 2002). While the younger children's answers were no less informative than the older children's, the group of very young children may have also found the language/structure of the questions difficult to comprehend as they were constructed for a reader not a listener. This process is also very time-consuming for a single researcher. As such, the interview style of data collection could distort any conclusions drawn in comparison with written responses.

Tools for data collection

Other tools used during the data collection phase of the project may include one or all of the following: surveys, artefacts, recording devices and interviews. Many of these strategies are discussed in detail in Phase 3; particularly those that require direct interaction with children. Here, we briefly discuss some of the key issues to consider at the design phase when planning to use these tools.

Surveys

Survey research applies to many forms of data collection including, open or closed question, anonymous questionnaire and self-administered questionnaire. Questionnaires are often chosen with older children, as they tend to feel relatively comfortable with this style of reporting and are more likely to complete a self-administered questionnaire.

Surveys are often chosen for data collection because of the ability of surveys to gain information from a large group of people in a relatively short amount of time. An advantage of survey design suggested by Burns (2000) is that it is an effective technique available to provide information on beliefs, attitudes and motives. Surveys can effectively elicit a spontaneous response from children without 'possible contamination' that can occur via other mediums of data collection. Anonymous surveys can often remove some of the perceived pressure on children to answer in a certain way. The children are able to engage, reflect and respond to each question at a level of their choosing, and with detail commensurate with their cognitive skills.

Artefacts

Wright (2001: 3) asserts from her work that 'drawing is one symbol system where children use imagery, often more fluently and articulately than they do language'. She uses the children's commentary to describe the presented pictures in her study. When collecting artefacts it is highly recommended that the children have opportunities to explain and provide a narrative to assist the researcher in their interpretation of particular works. Unfortunately it is often the case that researchers collect artefacts without an accompanying narrative. As such any analysis must be drawn solely from the content contained in the images. The absence of the author's narrative may well limit the identification of much of the meaning within each child's symbolic communication. It also compels the researcher to engage with each drawing with a purely observational eye. In addition, by offering children an opportunity to share their thinking through expressive languages, we are upholding their right to use whatever communication medium they feel most competent in.

Cameras and recording devices

Alison Clark (Clark and Moss 2001) uses child-taken photography extensively in her work using the Mosaic approach to participatory research with children. This is a relatively new approach to data generation and provides a method for both children and adults to be able to carefully examine what is going on from the child's perspective. Remember that when children take photographs of their environment, or other things that are important to them, they do so from quite a different field of vision than an adult-taken photograph or recording would capture. When children make their own recordings, whether photographs, video or audio documentations, they are playing an active not passive role in data generation. Alongside drawings and other artefacts, photographs and other digital recordings are providing rich and valuable data about the lived experience of childhood.

Interviews/focus groups

An alternative to a survey design is to conduct interviews or focus group discussions. However, when seeking the personal perspectives of children, any method that increases the child's interaction with another person may impact on their willingness to provide a deeply personal and thoughtful response (Minichiello 1999; Denzin and Lincoln 2000).

Engaging children in interviews may be considered, but should be discounted for any of the following reasons:

- The researcher does not have any personal relationship with the children and may present as intimidating, thus effecting the children's willingness to answer in an honest and open way.

- A pre-existing relationship may exist with the children such as their class teacher who intends to conduct the interviews may result in some perceived pressure upon the children, presenting a connotation of assessment (Hopkins 2002).

- Interviews can have a significant impact on the school's timetable, fewer respondents would be able to participate.

- Interviews remove the opportunity for some children to participate with complete anonymity (Minichiello 1999; Burns 2000).

Conversations with a purpose

Yet another way to view dialogues with children is to engage in what Deborah calls conversations with a purpose. Interviews and focus groups are particularly fraught with problems when working with very young children. By their very nature, the interview seems to have the connotation of something quite formal and thus intimi-dating to a young child. If you are engaging with children in a naturalistic setting, such as a preschool or school, one way of sharing ideas with which they are quite familiar is a discussion or meeting time. In a research context, this approach can work quite well in both larger and smaller groups, and is far less formal than an interview or focus group. Experience shows us that younger children are more comfortable with others around them for support, and are therefore more likely to openly engage in a discussion. Of course, as we have mentioned previously, the success of such an approach is highly reliant on the researcher's skill and a conversation partner with young children!

Ways to open research conversations with younger children might be:

'I was wondering about . . . and I thought you might be able to help me?'

'It has been a long time since I was a child and I have forgotten what . . . is like. Can you help me remember?'

'You know, I was thinking that since you come to school everyday, you must know so much about learning. I wonder if you could tell me about some of the things you do?'

'I heard from some other adults that children think . . . about . . . and I was wondering if that was true. What do you think?'

Over to you . . .

Jot down ways in which you might open your conversation with the children you hope to join in your project. What will be the best way for you to start?

Developing questions

When developing a survey, interview questions or conversation topics for children, it is important to ensure that the questions pose no emotional threat to their well-being. The questions should also be developed so that the children are likely to understand the structure, wording and intent of each question.

When considering the development of the survey, particular care should be taken in framing the questions to achieve responses that are least likely to lead the respondents to answer to please the researcher. As Neuman (2003: 276) states: 'Researchers sometimes want to find out whether respondents know about an issue or topics, but knowledge questions can be threatening because respondents do not want to appear ignorant.' This may hold true in an attitude survey, therefore it was important in structuring the questions so that they do not lead to a certain response.

As first impressions by respondents are important in survey work, the first few questions asked can determine the tone for the survey, and can help put the respondent at ease (Neuman 2003). When answering each question, participants, consciously or otherwise, are influenced by the answers they give of the preceding questions. The opening few questions, in general, should be easy to answer, never sensitive or threatening. For example, you might begin with questions relating to the personal activity or game preference, their favourite animals or foods.

The explanation before the completion of the survey is essential in order to put their minds at ease as to their freedom of expression and the confidentiality of the information they are being asked to provide.

Sensitive subject matter

Social research often asks respondents about difficult or uncomfortable subjects. Sensitive research involving children is sometimes a worthy activity. However, it is essential that significant care be taken, particularly with the skills of the researcher to conduct interviews or discussions with children. Before asking sensitive questions, you will have needed to develop a degree of trust and rapport with the children (Minichiello 1999; Hopkins 2002). However, due to logistical and time constraints, this may not always be possible. As such you should consider carefully the ethical standpoint of whether such a project should be pursued under less than ideal conditions.

It is essential that you as the researcher maintain a high level of sensitivity to the mood and behaviours of the children. This is especially relevant if the nature of the questions encourages the child with the flexibility to provide some very honest and personal information. When seeking personal information, you can never be sure what the children might share. Even if none of the questions are expected to be threatening *per se*, some children may provide answers that are of a sensitive nature and as such may elicit some unintended behaviour.

Recruitment

This is how you are going to go about requesting access to children through the gatekeepers or issuing the invitation to children to participate in your project. It is one of the most critical points in your project, as obviously you cannot proceed without your voluntary participants. Think clearly and carefully about how you are going to approach recruitment. Seek advice from other researchers who have worked with children in their studies, and ensure that you check the required ethical guidelines from your authorizing institution.

Ethical gatekeepers

While there is an apparent increase in the accordance of children's participation in research, this growth in participatory engagement could be jeopardized by perceived logistical barriers. It is important that researchers address these misconceptions before the gains of recent years dissipate in the name of research expediency. When preparing any research that involves human participants, in particular children and other perceived vulnerable groups, there are a number of ethical gatekeepers that need to be consulted. It is critical that you consider the process of developing the procedures and expected research activities from the viewpoint of ethical gatekeepers, and their standpoint on research involving children, both at the design stage and again during the conduct of the research.

Over to you . . .

Which gatekeepers do you see as critical in convincing that you have an ethically sound project proposal?

1.

2.

3.

4.

5.

Ethical clearance from stakeholders/participants

If your study involves research within schools, hospitals, clinics, sporting clubs and so on, the permission of institution/organization authority will be required, as will be the consent of all key personnel. If the study is conducted as part of a university study, it will be necessary to gain ethical approval from the University Human Research Ethics Committee (HREC) or similar. In almost all cases it will be a requirement to gain parental consent before approaching children to participate. Finally, but by no means least of all, it will be necessary to ensure that each child has provided their informed consent before participation.

Contact with schools and other institutions

You should, wherever possible, meet with or contact key personnel before beginning the formal processes of sending explanatory statements or information letters. In this way, you may well receive in-principle agreement and can rest a little easier knowing that you at least have some genuine interest in your project. You would then follow the protocols of ethical research and forward the appropriate information to the key personnel. By providing a full explanation of the research project (that has been cleared by your ethics committee), it is more likely that the key personnel you have made contact with will be helpful in liaising with other stakeholders, including staff and parents. In school-based research with children, the support of class teachers can be pivotal in providing available class time in order to conduct the study.

Parental consent

The recruitment of children and young people less than 18 years old for participation in a research project can be a particularly difficult task to complete in an authentically ethical way. Before any efforts to recruit the children can begin, their parents or guardians must first be fully informed of what you intend to do with their child. The parents of potential participants will usually be contacted via letter with information about the research project. While the parents are to be provided with a full written explanation of the voluntary nature of the project, it is most important that this information is written in a language that is clear and free of technical 'academic' language so that they will fully understand the aims and nature of the project and its contextual relevance. You will need to provide a concise overview of the project, including exactly what it is you expect from their child, how much time will be needed and the expected outcomes or benefits of your study. The child's parents will obviously have a special interest in the project and you should expect that some parents might make personal contact with you seeking clarification of the data collection process, and the purpose of the research.

Over to you . . .

- Who are the key personnel you might make contact with?

- How will you recruit your participants?

- Why will you recruit your participants this way?

Anonymity/confidentiality for the children

In most research contexts, particularly those conducted with children in schools, total anonymity is not always possible. Similarly, the notion of confidentiality at the research site can be difficult to achieve. Nevertheless, it is usually more appropriate to contextualize the project in terms of confidentiality. As such it is very important that the children understand the differences between anonymity and confidentiality. These distinctions are relevant, particularly when considering highly sensitive topics.

How the data is collected, that is, private interview, written survey, drawings, group discussion or video recording can also influence whether the children choose to participate. Many research projects allow for anonymity but throughout the process it is likely that there is potential for the participants to be identified. This may compromise the children's willingness to participate or provide full responses for fear of possible consequences. The storage of data after the collection phase can be a simple task but the context in which it is collected; for example, in classroom-based research, and poses other challenges.

The children should be fully informed prior to the project beginning about exactly who will have access to the information they provide, in what form; individual transcripts/ responses, or aggregated data with any identifying information removed. The children should be informed whether their teachers, parents or other adults with authority will know, hear or see what each person has to say. It is then of critical ethical importance that the researcher ensures that *only* those who have been nominated in the informing process are able to access the information.

Ponder this . . .

Jonathon was conducting a survey with a group of children during class time with the teacher and principal's assistance. The survey was asking the students opinions on issues that they might be concerned about in their class and school. Because of the possibility of some sensitive issues being raised, Jonathon assured the students that no one from the school would have access to the individual surveys to identify individual students. Half way through the session the principal entered the class and picked up some of the completed surveys that were placed at the front of the room and began reading. Jonathon approached the principal and reminded him that the responses were to remain confidential expecting the principal to respect the promised confidentiality and stop reading. The principal replied, 'they won't mind' and continued reading. Jonathon was concerned about how to respond.

During the process of explaining the project, the children should be informed about how, when and for what duration the information they provide might be shared with others. This would include forums such as conference presentations, journal articles, books, teaching events or seminars. In many cases the children do not realize that a researcher might be, for example, comparing one child's information or responses with other children from different places, times or within the same class. The information collected in one study is often referred to many times over. It may be used by other researchers conducting their own studies and, in the case of longitudinal work, would be referred to for many years.

While these considerations about the data may not seem particularly relevant at the time of the research, many participants do not fully comprehend the far-reaching and long-lasting potential use of their personally generated information. Respecting the personal integrity of the individuals and their role in the study should be paramount at all times and as such the children should be informed as early and as fully as possible.

Informing the adults about confidentiality

In institutional-based research it is often beneficial to seek the assistance of the staff to ensure that each child understands the voluntary nature of participation, and how the data will be collected and how it will be used. This process can also assist the centre's personnel in reinforcing the importance of confidentiality, and careful data management and their own need to step back from the data collection process, if not directly involved. Some of the case studies already presented here have shown where the potential conflict of interest between school/setting personnel and the children have occurred. The situations may be more easily resolved if the integrity of the data collection process is clearly and explicitly explained to all members of the school community.

Of course there is nothing to prevent the children themselves from informing the teachers of their input but this choice to share information should remain with the children at all times. In many cases you may effectively assure confidentiality but in some research scenarios, the children who are approached and willing to participate, may actively choose to remain anonymous. If your project does not prefer the anonymity of participants but such a choice can still be accommodated, you should honour this decision otherwise the children should be sensitively excluded from the study.

Ethics committees

When conducting research under the auspices of a university, hospital, clinic or other authorizing institution, clearance from the relevant ethics committee is essential. Each organization will be able to provide you with detailed guidelines and resources in relation to their particular process. It is wise for you to acknowledge and recognize that an ethics committee serves some important purposes including:

- the promotion of ethically sound research;
- fostering research that benefits the community;
- clarification of the responsibilities of institutions, researchers and review bodies;
- setting national standards for the conduct of ethical research;
- evaluating research.

The application process for ethical clearance provided by the relevant ethics committee should be used to guide the design, processes and procedures of your project and outline the continuing ethical conduct of your research. Some of the key issues that an ethics committee will expect you to have considered carefully prior to submission are that:

- You have had your project peer reviewed (i.e., it has been approved by your supervisor; a panel of experts has been convened for the purposes of reviewing research; it is the recipient of a research grant that has been awarded; it is commissioned research etc.).
- You have (or are in the process of seeking) permission from the authorizing person/s at the proposed research site, where relevant (such as an education department, a paediatric clinic, an elite youth sporting club etc.).
- You have (or are in the process of seeking) permission from the community elders or community councils, where relevant (such as an Indigenous Land Council).
- You have clear, plain language explanatory (or information) statements for gatekeepers and participants (explaining the why, how, who, when and where of your project).
- You have relevant and precise consent forms that are appropriate and specific for your participants.
- You have identified *in detail* the recruitment process.
- There is no conflict of interest evident, and if there is, you have clearly stated how this will be addressed.
- You have identified any risk (i.e. negligible risk, low risk, high risk, etc.) and how that risk will be mitigated.
- You have stated what burden will be expected of the participants (time, effort, inconvenience).
- You have stated what benefit the project will bring to the participants.
- You have identified if you are offering participants any incentives, and if so, why.
- You have addressed matters relating to information protection (remembering that it is virtually impossible to ensure confidentiality of information to a child under 18 years old due to the fact that consent must first come from a parent or guardian).
- Any legal issues have been identified and addressed appropriately.

It is important for you to be quite clear on the expectations of the ethics committee you are working with, and that you clearly address all of the requirements the committee needs in order to assess your project. Most ethics committees openly encourage a dialogue with researchers to ensure the approval process runs smoothly. When submitting work that involves children, you need to know what expertise is on the committee that is going to assist them in determining the ethical validity of your proposal. If you can foresee any gaps prior to submission, it is wise counsel to ensure you go that extra mile in your application so that you are painting a very clear and well-argued picture of your proposed work. In this way, you are less likely to run into difficulties and frustrations.

Ponder this . . .

Emma is a young doctor now studying for a Masters in Public Health who, in her spare time, coaches her younger sister's netball team. She also acts as the team doctor when the girls play away from their home courts. The team comprises young girls, 14–18 years of age who have been diagnosed as being on the Down's syndrome spectrum. Emma has submitted a proposal to her university's ethics committee to research the effect of obesity on young women with Down's syndrome. She intends to study the girls in her sister's netball team looking at their food choices, exercise regimes and the relationship between the two. She has said that there is negligible risk in the study and that there is no conflict of interest. She has also stated that she had a chat with her supervisor about the project and he said it was great. The ethics committee has come back to Emma with a number of issues that it states breaches the National Statement on Ethical Research. These include: 1) the fact that Emma's younger sister is in the cohort she intends to study; 2) the ability of young people with Down's syndrome to give informed consent; and 3) the fact that Emma has an established relationship with the cohort as their coach and sometimes team doctor. Emma is at a loss as to why these issues constitute ethical problems and why she should be expected to have to resubmit the application.

Peer review

There are a number of ways in which you can seek (or need to seek) the opinion of your peers in ensuring your project is ethically sound. You will be able to make a much stronger case for the imperative of your research if you can establish that you have received formal feedback, approval or funding for your project. This can take many forms, but it would be wise to ensure that a number of key aspects of your work have been critiqued. These should include, but are not limited to:

- conceptualization;
- methodology;
- research design and methods;
- currency of literature review;
- researcher's track record;
- capacity of the researchers to undertake the research project;
- any further training or support the researcher might need to ensure the project is successful.

Of course, if you have been successful in receiving competitive funding for your project, or if you have undertaken a university confirmation for your Ph.D., it is quite easy to demonstrate that your project has been peer reviewed. It is a little harder if you are undertaking a small piece of research such as a pilot study or an action research project in your classroom. You will need to find ways in which your proposal can be validated by a group of peers who have experience and expertise in evaluating those aspects mentioned in the list above. Unfortunately, getting the teacher next door to you saying it is a good idea will not make an ethics committee look favourably on your work, just based on this comment.

Institutional authorization

With research involving children becoming more prevalent, many sites are being identified as concentrated sources for accessing children and young people. These might include kindergartens or childcare centres, schools, sporting clubs, youth groups, church groups or particular precincts where children congregate. Other more specialized sites, where access could be problematic, might include hospitals, mental health clinics, refugee camps, detention centres, juvenile justice centres or rehabilitation facilities. For you to access children or young people in order to invite them to participate in your project, you will need to gain permission from the institutional authority. This might be as simple as the local school principal signing a consent form, or it may be a fully reviewed access process by the prison authorities if you are seeking the participation of very young children who are with their mothers in detention. Whatever the ease or not of the process, you will need to carefully consider how you will proceed in gaining permission, as without it your project will not be able to proceed.

Community elders, land councils or traditional owners

Increasingly, researchers are seeking to include children in research who are under the protection of community elders, land councils or traditional owners. In order to gain access to these children, you will need to consider carefully how you might present your proposal in a culturally respectful manner. In addition to this, many communities are feeling 'over-researched' so you may well have to make a very strong case to the custodians. The elders, the land council or traditional owners may have particular ethical issues that would need to be addressed in your project. These could be around gender, authority, particular issues that may not be discussed with outsiders, the place of children in the community or notions of cultural sensitivity. Try to find someone who can advise you before you approach the elder, land council or traditional owner. You may need to use a different protocol than you have done in the past. For example, it may not be appropriate to post an information letter and consent form. You may have to present it personally or through another person. The more time you spend on seeking advice and following protocol, the more likely your request will be agreed to.

Ponder this . . .

Alison was a very experienced researcher with children and had spent many years in her home country, England, refining her skills in this area. She was now confident that she could apply her skills to researching with children in other countries. She successfully applied for a grant to travel to Australia as she was particularly interested in understanding how young indigenous children viewed their well-being and she had never travelled to Australia so it was an attractive opportunity. She thought that a community in central Australia would be a good site for this study, as she knew there were a lot of remote indigenous communities in that area. Alison wrote to the Northern Territory Catholic Education Office with an outline of her study and they received it very enthusiastically. She was told she could approach any of the Catholic schools in the Territory. She followed this with an information letter and consent form to a small school near Alice Springs. The principal was also enthusiastic but did say that they had had a lot of visitors from universities in the last 12 months and his teachers would need to decide if she could work in their classrooms but did not see any problems in that respect. Alison was really excited and booked her ticket. She travelled to Alice Springs and that is where she found out that there was much more to working with children in an indigenous community than she had anticipated. She had not considered the fact that most of the children speak an indigenous language, and if they speak English it is not standard English. Nor had she given any thought to the historical tensions between the indigenous community and non-indigenous 'visitors'. Alison had not made any approach to community elders to seek their approval to work with the children, nor had she realized that a non-community member cannot stay in the township without permission from the governing authorities. In addition, the teachers were yet to give their approval for Alison to work in their classrooms. These among other issues seem to put Alison's project in clear jeopardy.

Parents

In a way, parents are also in a group we might refer to as ethical gatekeepers. Without the consent/agreement of parents, you will in most cases not be able to access children. There is some argument that researchers should be able to go directly to children: that children have the capacity to decide whether they will participate in a project or not. In some countries, such as Italy, universities do not require ethical clearance, and therefore it is quite possible to engage with children without parental consent. You will need to decide your own position on parents as ethical gatekeepers, depending on your country's approval processes and your own stance on including children in research.

Explanatory statements

Explanatory statements or information letters are the means by which you seek the informed consent of adults in order to gain access to children. These form a critical part of the ethical procedures that need to be in place prior to beginning your project. They will explain the why, how, what, when and where of your study in language that is accessible to the particular audience you are speaking to. Information letters can also be used to inform older children, but again, you need to use care in the type of language you use and that you can be sure that the child will understand what is being asked of them (see the next chapter on more about informed consent with children). The ethics committee that you are working with may have particular ethical aspects that they wish to be included in the letters, but generally speaking you will need to outline:

- your project title and your role (i.e., Ph.D. student);
- a brief explanation of the project and its aims and duration;
- which children you will be asking to participate (i.e., Year 4 children with glasses) and that their informed consent will also be sought;
- how much time you expect the child to be engaged with the research (e.g., each Monday morning for an hour) and what you expect them to do (discuss a topic in a group that will be digitally recorded);
- what risks there are and how they will be mitigated;
- how the child will benefit from participation;
- that participation is voluntary and that the adult or the child can choose to withdraw from the project at any time;
- how you will report back to the adults and children;
- contacts for the ethics committee and for you.

Ponder this . . .

Deborah has included a sample information letter from one of her recent projects for you to consider (Appendix 3). Some of the points of interest she would like you to note are that the HREC wished her to remove any reference to 'informed consent' in reference to the process of informing children. They firmly requested that the term 'informed assent' be used. They stated that this was in line with legal protocols for any person under 18 years old and distinguishes a minor from an adult. Deborah argues that this is in fact not the case and that children have the legal right to give consent. The legal definition of assent means to acquiesce whereas the legal definition for consent is to offer affirmative acceptance. For Deborah this is in line with her position of children as rights-holders in relation to research. In addition, the HREC requested that a less formal language be used when writing to parents, as they may not have the capacity to understand the contents. The director of the centre where the research was to take place responded that the language should be respectful and acknowledges parents' capacity as intelligent partners in education. She indicated that the centre did not, as a matter of policy, 'dumb down' language for parents. The letter in Appendix 3 is the original that was submitted.

Informed consent forms

With each explanatory statement or information letter you will need to attach a duplicate consent form: one copy for the participant/gatekeeper and one copy for the project file. As mentioned above, these consent forms may work well for older children, but you will need to rethink how you might document the consent of younger children. This will be discussed in the next chapter. Your consent forms need to be very clear in terms of what you are asking the person to agree to, particularly in terms of your methods of documenting their views/opinions/ideas and in terms of what might happen to the findings in the broader sense. So, you should include:

- consent-giver's name and, where applicable, their child's name;
- agreement that the participant has had any questions answered satisfactorily;
- agreement to participate or agreement for their child to participate in the project;
- agreement to have recording devices used (where applicable and please name these);
- agreement that the findings may be published, without identifying participants (where applicable);
- acknowledgement that the participants may withdraw at any time;
- space for signatures and dates (should be signed by participant and the researcher);
- again, Deborah shares an example of a consent form in Appendix 4 from the project described in the information letter (Appendix 3).

Regardless of the intentions of the ethical clearance process, many misconceptions can arise from the perspectives of the ethics committee and the individual researcher. The following attributions from the researchers' perspective sometimes emerge relating to ethics committees:

- extra layer of bureaucracy (Big Brother!);
- gatekeepers who don't understand – obstructionist;
- varied conceptions of children and childhood (theoretical vs. anecdotal);
- timeliness of approval process;
- understanding the intent of the research;
- heavy focus on quantitative methods 'not ethics-related';
- poor communication.

And, from the committee perspective:

- ethics committees are supporters of research;
- ethics committees have a duty to ensure ethical conduct;
- incomplete proposals will delay the process;
- methodologies must align with research question;

- researchers often present inappropriate consent/explanatory statements;
- the range/frequency of applications requires procedural fairness;
- with few specialist committees for child-related research, relies on the researcher as the expert to provide a clear proposal;
- poor communication of research aims.

None of the above issues are insurmountable and are often simply a consequence of poor planning on behalf of the researcher. Early and attentive planning and a philosophy of open communication should assure a positive experience with the committee.

Once a project enters the data collection phase, it is easy to think the ethical requirements are largely complete. You have clearance, which demonstrates you have considered the important issues of participation, consent and the merits of the project. You have completed your Researcher Capacity Analysis (RCA) and bolstered your team's membership and capacities.

While the formal requirements have been completed, the onus falls more heavily on you to maintain an ethical approach at this stage because for the majority of the data collection phase no one is watching. What is left to do but collect data? We now shift our discussion to the more practical aspects of conducting research with children.

Summary

This chapter has focused on:

- the key ethical deliberations when designing a research project that involves children;
- considerations of the roles of children in the research design;
- an overview of the main methodological styles in research that involves children;
- exploring the range of data collection tools and their ethical application;
- considering the researcher's strategic management of sensitive material;
- the process of recruitment, ethical clearance and the preparation of information and informed consent letters;
- the tensions present with anonymity and confidentiality;
- the role and perspectives of gatekeepers and ethics committees.

Phase 2 checklist

As you prepare to conduct the project, take a few minutes to gather your thoughts on the discussions presented in Phase 2. Consider how well prepared to conduct the study you are, where you need further work. The following checklist may assist.

Task	Complete Yes/No/In progress
✓ Identified the specific roles of the children in the project	
✓ Developed a methodological framework and communicated a clear philosophical alignment	
✓ Selected data collection tools that align with your chosen methodology	
✓ Developed appropriate, jargon-free interview/survey questions in a language appropriate for your participants	
✓ Identified and developed a selection of key communication strategies appropriate to the children's capacities	
✓ Developed strategies for addressing participant distress if dealing with sensitive subject matter	
✓ Considered how you will manage issues of anonymity and/or confidentiality	
✓ Prepared information and informed consent protocols both in letter form and as a verbal script where necessary, in language suitable for the target audience (i.e. parents, administrators, children)	
✓ Considered any unique cultural or community condition that may be present in your research context	
✓ Completed and submitted applications for ethical clearance for all relevant gatekeepers	

5

Phase 3 – conducting the research

Opening the conversation: inviting children as research participants

As we have seen so far, the international research community is beginning to develop a rich and substantial body of work around investigations with children. However, little of the research literature gives us detailed information on how to physically begin this work. Some researchers who have a background in working with children, such as teaching professionals, may have an advantage in engaging children in a research topic given their prior experiences in working with *groups* of children. Those who have less experience in daily interactions with groups of children, perhaps from the fields of sociology, health, community welfare, law or governance may well need some help and support in researching *with* children.

This would also hold true for those of you who are research students, or those who may be approaching this field of work for the very first time. This chapter, therefore, looks at some of the ways in which you can approach investigative fieldwork with children.

It has been proposed in Chapters 1 and 2 that significant knowledge about children and childhood can be generated when children's *active* participation in research is deliberately sought, and where their ideas, perspectives and feelings are accepted by adults as genuine and valid contributions. Alison Clark (Clark and Moss 2001; Clark 2005a, 2005b, 2010) from the UK is a leader in this field and has clearly demonstrated the worthiness of children's ideas and opinions for the exchange and debate of issues that affect children. So we must then ask ourselves, if children have traditionally found themselves in passive positions in the research process, how do they become active participators in matters that affect them? We must therefore approach our research in a way that it genuinely seeks to include children as active research participants and respects the skills that children can offer, looking for ways in which you can generate ideas and construct theories with the child.

Over to you . . .

Define what the active participation of children in research means to you. What should it look and feel like in practice?

Becoming familiar with each other

Imagine that you are asked to share detailed information about your experiences at work or university. This would involve you talking about your interactions with colleagues, classmates, lecturers, supervisors and other people you have daily contact with. You would also need to explain what you do during the day and perhaps evaluate these experiences. You might be videotaped, have your voice digitally recorded or you might be asked to write about your daily work. Once you have shared this information, it may find its way into a magazine, a journal, be presented to your colleagues, lecturers or supervisors, or even shared with your parents! Your views and opinions might make their way to an international forum such as a conference or seminar, attended by learned people in the field. While your ideas and opinions may be presented to others in a serious manner, people may find your views moving, they might find them confronting and they also might find them humorous with lots of hilarity ensuing.

Consider the trust the children are placing in you to be truthful in the reporting of their views and how that trust should be supported. Would you share your personal information with a stranger, someone you only met with once or twice? How different would the detail of the information be if you had developed a relationship with the researcher, over time? How truthful would you be with a relative stranger than with someone who had spent time with you, getting to know you and your peers?

The example of Sue (see p. 68) is not uncommon and reflects a lack of understanding of the recruitment process on her behalf. While in some cases, the one-off visit and explanation may suffice, in many circumstances it is essential that some time is taken to build a relationship with the children in order to 'sell' the project and its merits. If you see yourself as someone who works *with* children in research rather than one who works *on* children in research, it is critical that you dedicate time to establish a research relationship (or partnership) with the children. Many studies are now conducted over relatively short periods of time, due to budget or other constraints, which may impact on how meaningful the research relationship can be. Establishing trust and security with the children is, however, an important factor to consider when you ask them to agree to share their experiences, knowing that this sharing may then become part of a much wider and more public discussion. However, it is not so much an issue of 'how much time', but more your commitment to the quality of the conversation in developing the partnership – quality time (Harcourt and Conroy 2011).

Ponder this . . .

Sue, a researcher with some experience with children, has had her project approved by her university's ethics committee. After distributing the information letter to parents via the class teacher, she has now received back the signed consent forms from 15 of the 22 parents in the children's class she is conducting her research in. On her first day in the classroom, Sue decides her first task will be to get the informed consent of the children. She had not met the children previously. She spends about 15 minutes explaining her project to the children and how she would like them to be involved. She tells the children they can draw things for her and that she will tape their voices as they tell her about their drawings. Sue explains that lots of important people will hear what the children have to say. She then singles out the 15 children, whose parents have agreed, to also agree to participate in her project. Sue has asked the children to 'sign' their consent with smiley faces on individual forms she has preprepared. Only two of the children comply with this request. The rest of the children tell her they want to go and play. Sue is confused as she thought she was organized, friendly and explained things well. She is also worried and disappointed that the other children did not want to join her project.

Both adults and children need time to explore, reflect and understand what the complexities of working together as partners might be. Early discussion, where possibilities (and questions) are raised, by either the adults or the children, support the idea of having a shared meaning about what adult and child researchers will be working on together. When you create opportunities for children to consider the request to be involved in your research project (and what that might look and feel like), you establish and demonstrate one of the basic ground rules of a research relationship with children; that is, what you have to say; what you think about; is of interest to me.

Over to you . . .

Draw your research project timeline in the box. How much time have you allocated to getting to know the children and the research settings? What will be the impact of this timing on your relationship with the children?

We remind you here that children's capacities to agree to participate in research are contextual and relational (rather than developmental) and you must give thoughtful consideration to the specific context in which children are invited to participate. Familiar surroundings such as prior-to-school and school settings, or at home, may (or may not!) be optimal environments for you to initially talk with children. As these are everyday places and spaces where children live their childhoods, it also means that there can be opportunities for you and the children to establish partnerships around your research topic.

Whether the time frame for the research project is short or long, it is also a specific relationship that will probably end once the research project is completed. The temporary nature of this partnership must be discussed with the children and considered with sensitivity and respect. Being thoughtful about your engagement with the children in regard to moving in and out of their world, whether it is in a formal setting such as prior-to-school/school, or an informal setting such as at home should be something that is discussed with the children when you are informing the children and seeking their participation.

Engaging with the children

Integral to you moving towards developing research relationships with the children is beginning to know and understand how their world operates. Consider how (and when) you are going to introduce yourself, or be introduced, to the children. This introduction may well establish how your relationship with the children will proceed from that point on. Remember that not all children will be familiar with a university or other institution that you might come from and it will be helpful to provide a brief and simple explanation. You may also be the first researcher (or one in a long line!) that the children have encountered, so they may be in unfamiliar territory.

Over to you . . .

Using your current role and institution as a researcher, compose a brief introduction of yourself to the children at your local school who are:

1   a group of four-year-olds;

2   a group of eight-year-olds;

3   a group of 13-year-olds.

The physical context

Wherever possible, spend blocks of time observing the setting, whether it is a prior-to-school, school, home or other environment so that you are familiar with routines, timetables and transitions, the children's names, the kinds of activity they engage within their everyday lives, and how they interact with the adults (where relevant) around them. You are looking to see how a researcher might fit in to the particular setting and how your research project might make connections to the rhythm of the children's day. One of the key aspects of your familiarization foci should be on the kinds of communication tool the children use to express their ideas, thoughts, opinions and interests. This will be vital information when you are giving consideration to data collection methods and is a key element of acknowledging Article 13 of the United Nations Convention on the Rights of the Children (UNCRC), which tells us that children must be free to choose any manner of communication in order for their views to be heard.

Ponder this . . .

Kelvin has spent a week in the primary school classroom with the 10-year-olds he hopes might join him in his research project. He has noted that the children, notably the girls, seem to have a keen interest in drawing and reading. The girls also spend a large amount of time in smaller social groups, discussing issues (of life and other things!). The boys, on the other hand, do not seem to spend any length of time on drawing, reading or writing unless they are directed to, but do seem to enjoy 'mucking about' in twos and threes. Additionally, there are two newcomers to the classroom who speak very little English, which is the school's language of education. Kelvin wants to invite all children to share their ideas with him, but is now not sure what data collection tools he should use.

Informed consent

Once you have introduced yourself and familiarized yourself with the setting, you should now turn your thinking to what your expectations are of the participants (adults and children) in the research project. The children, within each research setting, should be offered a clear explanation of the why, what, when, where and who of the research process.

Explaining why

Share with children *why* you think this topic is important, for you and for them. Be very careful here in terms of what benefits might ensue. The aim of this type of research is to ensure that there is a benefit to children, as relates to their views and opinions, but you need to be clear in your own mind (as you should already be after the first two chapters) what the outcomes will be. For example, if you are researching children's ideas around high-quality outdoor spaces for children in the community, do you have the capacity to put in a swimming pool, if that is what the children tell you would add to the quality of life?

Over to you . . .

Of what benefit is your research project going to be

1   for the children who participate?

2   for children more generally?

Explaining what

Talk to the children about *what* it is exactly you are asking them to do. Are you just talking with them, are you wanting to videotape them, do you want them to fill out surveys or perhaps you want them to draw or write their responses. If you are intending to keep artefacts (e.g. a drawing) then the children need to know this. What will happen if a child wants to keep a drawing that you thought was for you to keep? How will you and the child negotiate this? Also consider the children's role/s in the analysis of your data. Are you going to revisit the data with the children? Will they have a role in the dissemination of the data? Do they have a right to veto what you might present in a more public forum?

Explaining when

You need to have a sense of how much time you will be spending in the children's classroom/home/context. This should have been negotiated when you were seeking research sites, but the children will not necessarily know this. Exactly *when* will you be there? Are you intending to come each Monday morning for three hours, perhaps you will be there each day for two months or maybe you will see them after school? Give the children a realistic expectation of your physical presence as well as what might happen if you cannot come.

Explaining where

Your familiarization visit should have given you an idea of how your project is going to fit in to the rhythm of life at the setting. In terms of *where* you might engage in research activity with the children, this can often be best negotiated with the children themselves. For example, Deborah has been working with groups of three- and four-year-olds over the past few years at the same prior-to-school setting and the big table in the foyer has become widely known by the children as the 'talking table'. This is where she gathers with the children to discuss matters relating to research. Older children may prefer a more private space, or the teacher/parent may have a preference as to where the discussions take place.

Your familiarization time should have given you an indication of the kind of language you would need to use to explain the project, its intentions and aims, to the children. Try to find words that you have noticed that are used in the children's everyday context. For example, children might work on 'projects' in art or they may 'investigate' in science. This strategy may make it easier for you to explain your research *project* and to establish a shared understanding about what the adult and children might do together. Here, using a common language, that which is already part of the classroom/context culture, assists in the development of a research relationship (Harcourt and Conroy 2011). It would also be useful to address terms not apparent in the children's vocabulary and explore these at this time. New words introduced for consideration in relation to your project can be discussed over as many sessions as necessary. Attempting to bridge the semantics of the academic world and that which the children inhabit becomes an important step. Through these dialogues, the adult and children will construct a shared meaning about the key terms that frame your project.

Consider this brief example of how the children deconstructed unfamiliar language in one of Deborah's studies (Harcourt 2011):

One new word introduced for consideration was 'quality' which was discussed over several sessions and one that the children finally decided had an association with the word 'good'. This decision was made only after careful consideration by the children who, while trying to construct their own understanding of the word quality, made reference to other aspects of their lives to establish its meaning. For example, Renee said, 'Do you mean Singapore Quality Class? My father says that means a good place to buy things.' And Celine said, 'I saw that word on a magazine from the supermarket. It means the stuff is good.'

Remember that children of any age need time to digest ideas and may need several meetings in order to clearly understand what it is that you are asking of them.

Over to you . . .

Write a potential script for explaining the why, what, when and where of your project to a group of six-year-old children in their second year of primary school. Consider what you know about six-year-olds and the kind of language they might be familiar with. Is your script going to be adequate for all children in the group?

Who will be invited

Now, take a moment here to consider *who* you are going to invite to participate in your project. Go back to Sue who only had 15 out of 22 parents of possible participants return their informed consent. You face several dilemmas here:

- How do you separate the children from those who have parental consent and those who do not? How will you explain this to the children?
- What will you do if a child who has parental consent but does not want to listen to your explanation?
- What will you do if a child, who does not have parental consent, wants to participate?
- Do all the children work with you at the same time? How do you make choices about who you work with and when?

Ponder this . . .

Jack (four years old) was building with blocks and decided to make a sign that said, 'Stop'. His intention is to stop the cleaners from dismantling his structure when they came in at night. Other children notice Jack's efforts in writing and decide that they too would 'write' signs to stop the cleaners and other children from destroying their block work. Judith has been observing the children's skill at 'writing' as a useful communication tool to express their ideas. She asks Andy if she could take a photo of his writing as he attaches it to his structure. Jack intercedes and says, 'This is my idea. Take a photo of my writing and me too'. Unfortunately, Jack's parents have declined to give their consent to participate. Andy's parents have agreed for him to participate. Judith is torn between wanting to acknowledge and recognize Jack's work in her project, but she knows his parents do not want him to take part in the project.

Extending the invitation

Once the information about the project had been carefully considered by all of the potential research participants, discussion can turn to extending an invitation to the children to participate in the project. It is critical at this point to reassure the children that their agreement to participate is important for your project to proceed, but that their initial agreement is not a one-off and final decision. It is therefore equally important that the children are sufficiently informed that a decision to withdraw their agreement, at any point in the project, would be respected without consequence. It is important to note here that many researchers may unconsciously use verbal and non-verbal languages of power, which can communicate to the child that they are expected to participate.

It is common for new researchers to the field to phrase requests to children to participate such as *I have come to get your permission* or *I have come to get you to sign saying you agree to be involved in my research* which may hold the intention to seek permission, but as you can see, the request is posed as an already negotiated agreement (Conroy and Harcourt 2009). The perceived authority of adults can imply power and many children may find it difficult or intimidating to decline the researcher's request. In an attempt to mitigate an imbalance of power, it would be useful to use the initial sessions with the children to discuss the research proposal, more generally, with the children as a group. This is an important step in your informing process and one that should be made equally clear to the adults in the setting as well, so that you avoid wherever possible any coercion that might occur.

Documenting consent

Once you are reasonably sure that the children are in a position to make an informed choice to participate in your project, you can move to the challenge of documenting their consent (and perhaps their dissent). Many children will be familiar with the notion of this type of documentation through the forms that go back and forth from school to home in relation to attending excursions and the like. For younger children, using these examples can contextualize what you are asking them to do. Our experience has shown us that even the youngest children have the competence to engage in this process. We share another example from Deborah's work (Harcourt 2011) with five- and six-year-olds:

> I showed the children the forms that parents might sign as examples of how an adult might record their permission. I considered these forms as providing the children with a reference point and another connection to familiar classroom practices. According to the teachers in both settings, children were familiar with excursion permission forms as part of the ritual of going out of the centre. They were invited to think of ways that they might record their permission. Since my journal had already become a familiar part of my activity in their classrooms, Hui Min (from Centre B) suggested it was the best place to write their permission (initially she was one of the dissenters). While all the others in her group agreed, I offered the same suggestion to the children in Centre A. The children were invited to record their names to indicate yes or no (as assent or dissent) in my journal. All 13 children from Centre A wrote their names and yes (15 April). Nine children (one was away) from Centre B wrote their names and yes (9 April). Three wrote their names and no. One, Alan, changed his mind that day (But I might change it back to no if I get tired). Each visit for several weeks was then begun with a confirmation of assent or dissent. In the week following initial assent, another child from Centre B who wrote no crossed it out and wrote yes (16 April). Four weeks later, the third dissenter (Hui Min) also changed her no to a yes (12 May).

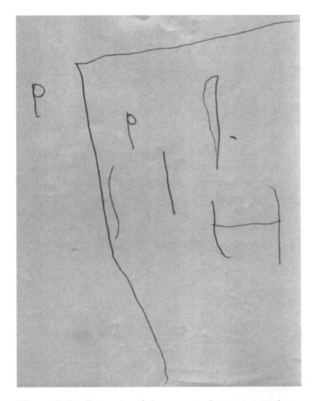

Figure 5.1   Example of documented agreement 1

There are many other ways in which children can document their agreement to participate in your project. For older children, completing surveys is considered to represent a person's consent. Should you wish then to use those surveys to prompt discussion groups, you would need to gain the more formal consent of the children involved. This might be done through a section on the bottom of the survey that asks for a contact email, or perhaps as a simple yes/no box for the child to agree to further engage with you.

When working with younger children, as the example above illustrates, you might need to spend more time co-constructing ways in which to document. Some examples of documented agreement can be seen in Figures 5.1–5.3. A three-year-old child was supported in his documentation by his older brother, who asked if he was happy to work with the researcher. The child wrote 'happy' as his agreement. The four-year-old children in one early childhood service decided that they could write OK as their agreement mark/signature as many were not able to 'sign', they suggested. They also decided that they would need to write OK (using a different colour) each time they agreed to work with the adults. A group of six-year-olds individualized their agreement with information about themselves as well as agreement. With this type of ownership over consent, the researcher can be reasonably confident that the children have understood the informing process and are genuinely interested in participating at *this point in time.*

Figure 5.2   Example of documented agreement 2

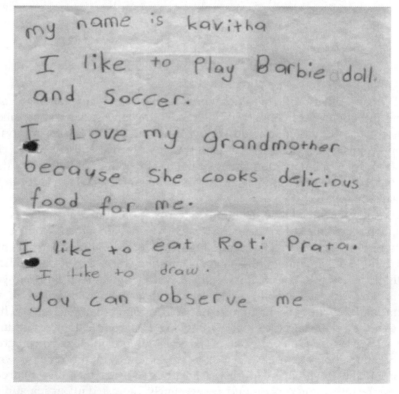

Figure 5.3   Example of documented agreement 3

Withdrawal of consent/opting out

In your explanatory statements or information letters, you have assured the gatekeepers that anyone involved in the project may withdraw their consent at any time, without consequence. You will have also spoken to the children about this, but it could be difficult for them to realize the actual action/s that they might be able to call upon to withdraw or opt out. For very young children, it is the researcher who will have to identify what this might look and feel like.

As noted in the example above where children opted in over several weeks, the same could apply to opting out. You will need to consider how you will mark this process. In the case of the children writing their names and *yes* in the research journal, they may be able to cross out the yes and put a *no*. In other projects, Deborah has invited children to join in research conversations on a session-by-session basis, and children have chosen whether or not they wished to join in at that time. Some children have suggested they are 'too busy at the moment' and may have time to join in the next time, while others have just said 'no', without any explanation. A four-year-old girl, who was visibly upset when her mother dropped her off at preschool, was invited to join in a discussion. She said 'no' to begin with. A few minutes later she said she probably would come, but the researcher would need to give her a cuddle if she got sad as she wanted to stay home with her Aunty who was visiting. Very young children may look or move away from the researcher, cry, cling to a more familiar adult or indeed just fall asleep! Older children may hide out of view when key observations are being taken, actively disrupt interviews by not answering questions or may interrupt other participants. In all of these actions, children are showing their disinterest in the research and in this way, children are empowered to opt in and out as they feel inclined.

When children decide that they do not want to participate at any given time, or indeed ever again, it can cause significant disruption to your progress. For example, you will need to consider the impact on data that you have already collected, which may need to be discounted; withdrawal of children will affect your sample size and you may need to recruit other children; the integration of data of the child/children who withdraw with other consenting participants will need to be carefully considered. At all times, you will need to keep at the forefront of your decision-making, the maintaining of an ethical stance.

Including all children

Now that many researchers are becoming more familiar with research *with* children, as an approach to actively involving children in research, we are turning our thoughts to how we might engage in an authentic way with children who may find themselves marginalized through more traditional approaches to research. We are seeking ways in which we might be more inclusive of children's voices, in an attempt to provide authentic spaces for all children to be heard (wherever possible) as is their right under the UNCRC.

We begin with infants and toddlers who are yet to develop the language that would assist you in explaining the project and gaining their informed consent. If you do not have a lot of experience with infants and toddlers, this might seem a daunting task. Regardless of how old a child is, they are viewed under the UNCRC as having the competence to share their views and opinions on matters concerning them. So how do you engage with a 12-month-old child?

Ponder this . . .

Jeremy is seeking to understand the soothing effects of music on very young children when they are going to sleep. He has the permission of the parents of five infants to video-record the children as they are put down for a nap at day care, while classical music is being played. Jeremy has noticed that while three of the children seem at ease in his presence, allowing him to play near them, responding to his conversations with smiles and utterances, two of the children cry and seek the comfort of their familiar carers whenever Jeremy enters the room. He also notices in his observations that when it is time for the children to go to bed, they can be quite irritable and unsettled. Jeremy recalls his university professor discussing the non-verbal cues that infants give, including body language they may use around strangers when they are distressed or wary. His professor also mentioned that infants can be upset when very tired, which can be exacerbated when there are more than one or two adults in close proximity. He is keen to ensure that the children, as best as he can gauge, are happy for him to continue his study.

Similarly, when attempting to include children with disabilities who you believe may not have the capacity to consent; perhaps you see children with autism or children with severe cognitive delays in this light, and it all may seem quite a challenge. However, their disability should not impact on their right to have an opinion in matters that concern them. They are children first, and the disability should be a secondary consideration (Harcourt and Sargeant 2011). Colleagues have found that forming a strong relationship with the child's/children's primary carers and/or teachers is a critical aspect of ensuring the child is happy for you to a) be near them, b) observe them and c) engage them in your project. You will rely heavily on the people closest to the children to help you interpret meaning and to help you understand what the child is communicating to you.

Watching how the parents/primary carers/teachers interact with the children, spending time with the children so that they become familiar with your presence, being seen by the children exchanging conversation with their parents and carers/ teachers, and observing the ways in which the children communicate are all important strategies when working with children who might often find themselves in the 'too hard box'. In this way, you are more likely to be successful in engaging with these children and able to defend your notion of agreement to participate by these children.

Over to you . . .

You are about to undertake a three-month study with nine-year-old children in Berlin, where you have only visited once and where you do not speak the language. What do you need in your 'tool kit' in order to engage with these children?

Researching across languages, cultures and unfamiliar contexts

One aspect of research with children that is becoming more frequent is collaborating with colleagues across countries and across cultures. Both Deborah and Jonathon have had experience in conducting projects in Sweden and Deborah has also completed projects in Italy. While they can get by at a rudimentary level as far as language is concerned, it is not enough to sustain research conversations with children. While this type of research is very rewarding and makes a significant contribution to our understandings of children and childhood on a more global level, it can be quite complex. For example, translating ideas back and forth across two languages is time-consuming and something that many children may not be familiar with. It is also fair to say that the meaning of a word in one language may not be the same in another. For example, when repeating the study on quality, mentioned earlier, which was first conducted in Singapore where the children said quality meant 'good', in the second study conducted in Italy the children decided the word for quality was 'importante' (important). Your familiarization process then can take on a much wider scope and must include your relationship with a translator, whether that be a fellow researcher (preferable) or a fellow academic who is happy to assist in the process but is not involved in the project (second best) or you may be working with a pure language translator (avoid if you can unless they are used to this type of work).

Opening the research conversation

Finally in this chapter, we come to actually beginning the research conversation; that is, data collection with the children. With a commitment to collaborating with the children on as many aspects of the study as possible, you might seek ideas from the children on how the adult and child researchers might find out about the particular topic you are investigating. Deborah shares an example of opening a research conversation with five-year-old children:

> I used the provocation; I wonder how I might find out about a good school? You see, I have forgotten what it is like to go to school. Since we know each other a little bit, maybe you could help me? I noted that many children were enthusiastic offering; You need to ask lots of questions to us, while others were more reticent in their responses, listening rather than contributing verbally to conversations. In later discussions, the groups talked about how the information might be collected (e.g. Maybe we could write or draw for you?) and what might happen to it once it was given to me (e.g. I need to show it to other people at the University where I work. Sometimes I will share your ideas with other teachers who work with children or who do research like us).

Beginning with the notion of your central research question it is possible for you to follow conversation threads with children around topics related to the question. It is important that the children are able to lead the conversations, and therefore be empowered to weave in the aspects of the topic they feel important to share with you. This approach can bring some surprising elements to conversations, and ones that were perhaps you have initially not considered as being noteworthy for children. From the many conversations you are likely to have with the children and the amount of data that is generated, you will note similar themes emerging, and these can then be used as the basis for analysing the data.

Ponder this . . .

> Jennifer's university ethics committee has stipulated that she is to protect the identity of her participants by giving them either pseudonyms or using the likes of 'Child 1' to denote children in the project. Towards the end of the project, Jennifer was discussing this matter with the six-year-old children she has been working with. 'What are you going to be called in the writing Jennifer?' asked Toby. 'I will be called Jennifer,' she responded. 'Then I want to be called Toby because that's my real name and I want people to know who I really am,' he replied.

A note on privacy

Two things we would like you to consider at this point. When you are informing the children about the project, you need to discuss with them what they might do if they had something to share about someone or something that was not so kind or good. You have a legal and ethical responsibility to ensure that no harm comes to the children, and each jurisdiction has protocols in place in terms of reporting these things. The children need to know this. In addition, other things that children might share might be hurtful or embarrassing to them or others and you need to ask them to tell you when it would be OK to use it in the project or when it should not be written down, recorded or taken away. The second point has been alluded to in the 'Ponder this . . .' box above. If we consider children to be valid informants who can clearly and effectively report on matters pertaining to children and their childhoods, why should we insist upon changing their names to a letter, number or name that does not acknowledge their particular contribution. We leave you here with that thought.

Summary

This chapter has focused on:

- opening the conversation: inviting children as research participants;
- engaging with the children in their context;
- the process of gaining informed consent through key explanations and the documentation of children's agreement;
- recognizing and providing children with the options to withdraw their participation and consent;
- considering the multiplicity of children and the implications of research with children with diverse abilities, cultures and contexts;
- the importance of maintaining a respect for children's privacy.

6

Maintaining ethical practice

Introduction

Up to this point the main focus of the research project has necessarily centred on preparing a valid and reliable study that advances knowledge and achieves benefit to the children involved. In gaining approval to conduct the study from the key stakeholders, gatekeepers and authorities, the justification for your study will have been presented. However, once the data collection phase begins, the responsibility for ethical conduct as a researcher rests with you. Not only is an awareness of what ethical conduct looks and feels like important, putting that knowledge into practice in a consistent manner is essential.

Ponder this . . .

Jenna was working with a group of 10-year-old children who were talking about aspects of learning at school. She had submitted a proposal to an international educational research conference, which perhaps overstated her initial findings. The conference was in one month's time, and as yet, she did not really have any data that she thought had the 'wow' factor necessary to engage her conference audience, or that demonstrated the worthiness of her study. She really wanted to impress at the conference as she was up for promotion at the end of the year and needed some strong feedback from her anticipated audience of experts in the field of research with children. The children were not co-operating and to make matters worse, the principal of the school kept coming in to check up on what she and the children were saying. Jenna had some old data from another study that, with a bit of tweaking, could pass as relevant to this current study. She thought she just might go down this path as a solution.

Ethical conduct

Across the globe, key research organizations have codes of ethical conduct by which they expect researchers to abide. For a range of reasons many researchers are unaware of the detail of these codes or may not fully understand how they might be applied in practice. Two examples of research codes of practices are presented below, but there are many across the world that all share common principles, most of which are addressed throughout this book.

In Australia, for example, researchers are governed and guided by the Australian Code for the Responsible Conduct of Research (Australian Government 2011: 2) which states:

> The Code is written specifically for universities and other public sector research institutions. However, all organisations involved in research will be encouraged to incorporate it as far as possible in their operating environments. The Code is also a reference for people outside the research community who require information on the standards expected in responsible conduct of research within Australia.

Another example is from the UK where the UK Research Integrity Office (www. ukrio.org) presents a Code of Practice for Research that is guided by six key principles: Excellence, Honesty, Integrity, Cooperation, Accountability, Training and Skills, and Safety. More than 50 Universities in the UK have adopted this code.

In essence, these ethical codes are in place to ensure researchers maintain high standards of responsible research. Researchers must foster and maintain a research environment that demonstrates intellectual honesty and integrity and, scholarly and scientific rigour. In order to uphold these codes, researchers are advised that they must:

- respect the truth and the rights of those affected by their research;
- manage conflicts of interest so that ambition and personal advantage do not compromise ethical or scholarly considerations;
- adopt methods appropriate for achieving the aims of each research proposal;
- follow proper practices for safety and security;
- cite awards, degrees conferred and research publications accurately, including the status of any publication, such as under review or in press;
- promote adoption of the codes and avoid departures from the responsible conduct of research;
- conform to the policies adopted by their institutions and bodies funding the research.

Over to you . . .

What are the key elements in your study that you will need to ensure you keep at the forefront of your ethical conduct?

There are several key points that you might like to think about here. As we have said before, ethical dilemmas that arise in a study with children are not going to be immediately evident when you set out. They often happen or unfold at unexpected moments, so it is best to try to consider how you might address some of the most common. We will try to highlight some of the issues that we have faced, but of course there will be many others.

> ### Over to you . . .
>
> A child really wants to be involved in your project but the parents have not given their consent. What should you do?

There was an example of this mentioned earlier, and it is a common issue in our experience. You must abide by the consent of the parents and try to explain this as best you can to the child. You may speak to the teacher or other guardian of the child to see if it might be appropriate to ask the parent to reconsider. In one project Deborah was involved in, two children were generating data alongside other children, but it was not going to be included in any aspect of the research. However, the children in the project were making a book and both non-parent-consenting children wanted their work included. The director of the preschool suggested that a mock of the book was shown to the parents to see if they would object to these inclusions. They agreed when they could see how proud their children were of their contributions.

> ### Over to you . . .
>
> A boy of 11 years of age becomes clearly agitated in the small group conversation group. What can you do to support him?

It does happen. Even in the most seemingly unobtrusive projects, children can become distressed. In fact, it may have nothing at all to do with the project but such disruptions can cause significant difficulties in progressing the research. You must have a contingency plan in place should children show *any* signs of being upset or uncomfortable when participating in your project. An ethics committee will have expected you to identify an appropriate person to provide comfort or counselling to children in this situation. It is wise not to just do this as a 'tick and flick' procedure, but to ensure that such a person would be on hand if needed. This will be particularly necessary if you are investigating a sensitive issue, or if you are working with children or young people in institutionalized care or detention.

Over to you . . .

A child divulges that he has engaged in an illegal activity. What do you need to do next?

You will have assured the children that what they tell you will be kept confidential or 'off-the-record' should they so wish and, therefore, this is a very tricky situation. If your research question has specifically set out to capture statistics or narratives on this type of activity, such as under-age drinking, then you would need to uphold the confidentiality of the information. You would need to use your discretion should your research focus not be about examining illegal activity. There will be statutory requirements for mandatory reporting in some states/countries and you will be obliged to adhere to these laws. This would apply particularly if a child's well-being is being put at risk, such as in abuse or neglect situations. At the very least you should confer with the teacher or guardian in raising your concerns.

Ponder this . . .

Edward is a sole researcher engaging with a group of 15-year-olds at a single gender school. Ed's topic is about young people's decision-making processes around commencing sexual activity. The teacher has decided that it will be OK for Ed to take three of the students over to the sports hall to conduct his interview as it will be much quieter as there will be no one to disturb them. Ed thinks it would be quite good to have a quiet talk with these students away from the prying eyes of the class teacher.

One of the suggestions given in the previous chapter was to spend some time with the children to find out what communication tools they use in everyday situations to ensure that your data collection methods are in line with what the children are competent at. There is no way that you should be enforcing a data generation method on children, for your own benefit, if they do not like communicating their ideas in this way. Rich data can be generated in a broad range of ways when you are working with children in research and it is your responsibility to ensure that you are using methods that are best suited to your participants.

Over to you . . .

You really want to use drawings as one of the data collection methods because they look good in publications, but the five-year-old boys do not like drawing. How will you proceed?

As has been suggested, once the formal ethical approval has been granted, it really is over to you to ensure that you maintain ethical standards throughout the rest of the research process. While the data collection phase could be said to be a critical period for ethical dilemmas to arise, once this is over it is *not* time to rest easy and think ethics has been taken care of.

Including children in the analysis of data

One of the key features of researching with children is that you are attempting to gain an insight into the thoughts and ideas of children. At times you can be presented with sometimes very personal and detailed information on the lives of the children who participate in your projects. The process of analysis and reflection may then cause you to engage in some deep reflection as part of the process of making sense of the data. You cannot always be sure that what you think the children meant by a particular comment or data set is, in fact, a true representation of their contributions. By including the children during the transcription and analysis phase of the study such misinterpretations are less likely to occur.

Involving children in the analysis of data means that you will be taking your commitment to children's participation further along the path of authentic engagement. In your planning, you will need to consider how this will be done and what extra time and effort will be needed to be set aside in order to achieve this. There is no one way to approach this process, but we would like to offer a couple of examples from our own work that seem to have worked well for us.

Example 1

Deborah often uses drawings and narratives with young children in preschool settings as a means of documenting their ideas and opinions on a range of matters. The narratives that accompany the drawings are always written (in pencil) on the back of the drawings by Deborah and/or her adult co-researchers. Once the child has shared their thinking, the adult reads the script back to the child and asks questions such as 'Did I write all of the words that you wanted to say?' or 'Is this exactly what you said?' or 'Did I write this in the right way for you?' The child is always asked if they wish to change or add anything. Children will often correct the narrative or ask for parts to be taken away. They may also think of additional pieces of information to add.

Example 2

Much of Jonathon's research with tween children, those between 8 and 12 years old involves visiting children, usually at school and inviting them to complete a questionnaire about their emotions and their views of the future. The questionnaire consists of open-ended questions that take some time to transcribe and prepare for analysis. In addition each response is written in each child's own style, so no two responses will necessarily be identical which is unlike other forms of survey. After the responses have been analysed off site, Jonathon pays a return to the participating students to report back on what his analysis revealed. This main reason for the second visit is to allow the children to confirm, question or amend anything they feel is being misrepresented. These sessions allow for an authentication of the analysis process that the children were not able to participate in and often provide valuable added insights that inform Jonathon's work.

Example 3

Another example that Deborah can offer is around naming the themes that might serve to identify a data set that was generated over a lengthy period of time. The adult researcher had loosely grouped drawings, narratives and conversations into categories that appeared to be about curriculum, peer relationships, teaching and learning, and physical environments. Several examples of the children's work in each category were offered back to the children with a question such as 'What do you think all of these ideas are about?' In fact, the children named curriculum 'That's about learning'; peer relationships became 'Oh, that is all about friends'; teaching and learning 'That's about our teachers Ms X and Ms Y'; and the final theme physical environment became 'Inside and outside'. In this way, the children became engaged as more than just data generators, but a genuine part of the analytical process.

During the collection of the data and again in the preparation of the data for analysis, the researcher can identify whether the participants have embraced the experience and taken the opportunity to state their views and opinions. Observations made in the field by the researcher can be reinforced or disputed by the individual and collective views emerging in the data. Such individual and/or collective convergences and differences expressed can present a challenge in any reporting of results where the voice of the individual and/or collective can be lost. Such is the importance of providing children a right to correction where possible.

Right to correction

Relevant child-related research presents professional communities with a strong foundation for innovative, progressive and valid evidence for consideration. This foundation provides us with an opportunity to challenge common beliefs about children and childhood and to improve child-related professional practices. To achieve this, however, it is imperative that the integrity or trustworthiness of a study is maintained. Change will not occur merely because research suggests it should, no matter how much evidence is put forward. The argument presented by research findings must be both compelling and irrefutable. In seeking to effect changes in attitudes, knowledge and practice, it is imperative that researchers seek to affirm the accuracy of their analysis by revisiting the data source (the children) where possible.

Many research commentators suggest that unequal power does not just disappear when children who have reached a certain age are involved. It can be said that even 16-, 17- and 18-year-olds are rarely given the opportunity to discuss ethical implications, contribute to data interpretation, provide reflections on the data or have input on policy implications. By virtue of the presupposed hierarchical relationship between adult and child, any power given or removed from children remains at the sole discretion of the adult. Such imbalances can be extended through parental coercion; stakeholder positions of what might be 'in the child's best interest' or research that is deemed too sensitive for young children to be discussing. These powerful adult decision-makers can either block or enable research activity on behalf of children and young people. When children are given opportunities to be heard, adults often express their surprise or astonishment at the sophisticated responses provided by children, which unfortunately reinforces the hierarchy of expectation.

To have some control over how other people see us, or how others portray us, is an inherent right afforded to many adults but rarely offered to children. Children have no right of correction, particularly in relation to the stereotyping of their capacities and competence and of childhood more generally. Children are often not debriefed after a study due to an emphasis on group trends rather than individual cases as the participants are often treated as objects of a study or informants, rather than active participants. It has been our experience that including children in the processes of verifying the data has been a very positive experience. In fact, most children relish the opportunity to state their view and have it accepted as worth while and valuable.

Denzin and Lincoln (2000) assert that in the context of the qualitative research paradigm, where our type of research resides, trustworthiness is a more appropriate construct than the notion of validity. The use of this research paradigm is oriented towards the production of a reconstructed understanding of children and childhood from which we attempt to draw meaning from the data generated. The interaction between the researcher and the children through analysis and interpretation allows a co-constructed meaning to emerge. Meaning is of particular importance in studies that involve children, as the specific features influencing the lifeworlds of children need to be acknowledged. This acknowledgement recognizes not only the uniqueness of the child and their own experience but also the influences brought to the analysis by the (adult) researcher's perspective.

Summary

This chapter has focused on:

- the importance of maintaining ethical conduct throughout the project and maintaining a level of self-regulation;
- identifying the possibilities of including children in the analysis;
- the importance of offering children right to correct any information they have provided to you.

Phase 3 checklist

As you prepare to conclude the project and share your results with the wider community, consider how you conducted your research within a framework of ethical practice. The following checklist may assist you in identifying some areas for consideration in your next research endeavour.

Task	Complete Yes/No/In progress
✓ Provided an invitation to the children to participate using language that encouraged their full participation	
✓ Participated in the 'life' of the setting without imposing or overly disrupting the regular routines	
✓ Communicated the duration, need and relevance of the study to the children clearly while including all relevant information regarding yours and their expected involvement	
✓ Documented all consent and provided regular reminders to the children of their freedom to withdraw at any time	
✓ Conducted data collection that respected the autonomy, safety and wishes of participants at all times	
✓ Maintained confidentially in data collection and management at all times	

Task	Complete Yes/No/In progress
✓ Responded appropriately at times if children experienced distress or appeared disinterested. Offered appropriate support	
✓ Offered the children the opportunity to confirm or correct any results and recordings of conversations	
✓ Sought clarification from the children regarding any ambiguous information	
✓ Maintained a professional distance at all times	
✓ Invited, considered and included children's perspective on the project and its conduct	
✓ Adhered at all times to the requirements detailed in the ethics approval documentation	

7

Phase 4 – dissemination of your work

Introduction

In many projects, once the data has been collected and analysed, the attention of the researcher turns to disseminating the knowledge gained to a wider audience. Communicating the results of the study can take many forms and may well occur over an extended period of time after the project concludes. In many cases the children will have moved on from the context in which they were studied, some will have relocated, while others will have simply 'grown up' and moved to another stage of their lives not relevant to the study. Simply put, the children who contributed to the study may not be children anymore and will not directly benefit from any development that may emerge as a result. Regardless of where the children of the study are now situated, the ethical conduct of the research does not end. The process of honouring their participation through the communication and enduring publication of your results remains an important consideration.

The results of your study may be communicated through a range of forums including conferences, seminars, online blogs and video sites, academic and professional journals, and books and in teaching materials. The study might receive interest from the media and through this medium the results may be presented in television news programmes, newspapers, through radio and online news services. How your information is communicated and interpreted is, in some cases, beyond your control so it is critical that what you do publish is both accurate and reflective of the key results of your study. What you say to the wider community about your study should at all times correlate with what you told your participants would happen.

Over to you . . .

- What is your potential five-year dissemination plan for your current study?

- Conference/s:

- Journal publication/s:

- Book chapter/s:

- Professional magazine/s:

- Grant application/s:

- Teaching/professional material:

- Other:

Reporting back to the participants

The written language used for a journal is necessarily different to that of a book and again will be more simplified when communicated to the general public in the media. As such, each time your results are presented, the anticipated audience must be at the forefront of your consideration. Before wider dissemination of your results, it stands as a professional (and ethical) courtesy that, where possible, you first present your result and conclusions to the participants. In alignment with the informed consent processes that you developed for the children involved in your research project, your results should be shared with them in forms appropriate to their capacity.

While more research now considers the child's view and includes more child voice at the preparation and data collection phase, there remains a paucity of research that provides feedback directly to the participants. When considering the communication of your conclusions to the participants bear in mind the following prompt; 'for whom am I writing?' The communication of your results to the participants must be in a form that is of value and appropriate to their context. Writings that are overly academic can create suspicion and discontent in children's attitude to adults and possible future participation in research.

Ponder this . . .

As part of the data collection phase of her Ph.D., Sarah has spent one school year with a group of five-year-old children examining how they measured the quality of their prior-to-school experiences. Sarah was required to begin dissemination of her results as part of her learning and engagement with the academic world. She had some very interesting data and was pleased that her abstract had been accepted for an early childhood research conference in Europe. Sarah explained to the children that she wanted to share their ideas and opinions about their experiences and that she had put together a PowerPoint presentation of their work together. She organized a session where she showed the children her presentation as she wanted to be sure she had constructed an accurate overview of the children's ideas. At the end of the presentation, one child said to her, 'You can't tell people those ideas. They are ours. We will have to come with you otherwise it's not fair.' Sarah was at a loss as to what to do.

A word on ethical presentation at conferences and seminars

One of the immediate ways in which to achieve getting your work out to a like-minded audience is through conferences and seminars. These provide a forum for feedback on work that you may be considering publishing in a journal, as a book or book chapter. They are also a way of disseminating new research methodologies, methods or results that may take some time (up to a year or more) to get into a published version.

Think carefully about what you will be presenting about the whole process of your research with children. Your role in disseminating your work is to educate others about, not only ways of conducting this type of research, but also ways of conducting ethical, respectful and honest research. Think about what you may say about:

- how you conceptualized your project and how children influenced this process;
- what methodology guides your work and children's role in that process;
- how you went about informed consent with the children and the opting in/out processes;
- how you decided on data collection methods with a view to the children's communication competences;
- what role children had in the data analysis and why;
- how children influenced the decisions around dissemination;
- the context of your presentation or writing.

Ponder this . . .

Anne was in the audience as an interested participant at a well-regarded early childhood research conference. She had been writing and presenting her own work with young children and was expecting to gain new knowledge around this research field. She had chosen to go to a self-organized symposium entitled 'Listening to children in research' which was being presented by a group of leading academics in the field of early childhood. So, she was sure it would be a good learning experience. The first presenter offered the participants her thinking on conceptualizing research with children, basing it on the United Nations Convention on the Rights of the Child (UNCRC), the sociology of childhood and image of child. She spoke about respecting children's right to a voice and their right to active participation in research. The children in her project, which was a government-funded project, were clearly informants (data generators) only. The second presenter talked the audience through her way of informing children about her project. She used a puppet to tell the children about the project and asked them to tell the puppet if they agreed to participate. The third presenter put up many narratives and pictures from the children in her project which had the audience laughing, and making comments such as 'how cute' or 'isn't that sweet'. Anne left the symposium very disappointed with what she saw and heard. She had expected that the children involved in the projects would have been held in high esteem as research partners, that the rhetoric around Articles 12 and 13 of the UNCRC would be upheld in practice, and that children's views and opinions would be presented in such a manner as to ensure that they were positioned as serious contributors to research conversations.

Much of the recent research that includes children's voice and participation serves dual purposes. First, it disseminates the results of the core research project and, second by providing exemplars as to how to include children at all stages of the process that can inform both the researcher and the research project. Such research outcomes reveal a re-emergence of the hermeneutic tradition in the participatory research methodologies being applied with children (Gadamer 1976).

Summary

This chapter has focused on:

- the importance of reporting your findings back to the participants at the conclusion of the study;
- considerations of who, where and how your results will be communicated to the research community and general public.

Phase 4 checklist

Phase 4 represents a culminating series of activities relating to your research project but the ethical considerations here are no less important. Consider the following checklist to assure that your project is concluded with the same ethical imperatives in which it began.

Task	Complete Yes/No/In progress
✓ Provided a report, in an appropriate format and language, whether written, video, oral presentation directly to your research participants	
✓ Considered the most appropriate forums for communicating your results in professional and public domains	
✓ Respected the privacy and confidentiality of the children and the context when reporting your results	
✓ Provided a model of ethical research practice for other researchers seeking to engage with children in their work	

Concluding remarks

This book has been conceived in order to address many of the ethical issues that researchers have confronted over the past 10 years in their work with children. We have attempted to extrapolate the key elements for ethical consideration that we believe need to be examined by any researcher undertaking this important work. We have drawn upon both contemporary and historical conceptualization tools to guide our thinking and have shared some of the less travelled paths for considering children as research participants.

An ethical consideration should override a methodological consideration. An ethical response to a situation *must* always come before any other consideration in your work with children. We therefore began this book with a declaration of our intent to provoke consideration, reflection and a systematic approach to doing ethical research with children. At this point in our endeavour we anticipate that you have at least begun this exploration, or perhaps even reconsidered your position, and now hold a richer perspective of the ethics of researching with children. What is crucial at this point is that you are being reflexive: reflexive as a researcher, as an educator, as a co-constructor of knowledge, as a data documenter and generator, as a disseminator, as an advocate and activist. We trust that you are beginning to appreciate the complexity of ethics in research with children and the need for an ethical stance to permeate all work you do with, or even considering doing with, children.

Throughout this book we have reinforced the importance of recognizing and listening to children as competent activists, and are optimistic that to some extent, based on the evidence provided and from your own experiences, that you share this perspective. Children have a central place and space in any work that is considering children and childhood. As a member of a research academy, you have a moral, ethical, social and political obligation to share your work in order to demonstrate the deep commitment we all have to ensure that the children inhabit a respectful place and space in research. An ethical perspective is not about flawless conduct, but about reflective conduct, it is about planning, anticipation, expectation and respect for children. Combining and applying these elements to your research will result in a more fulfilling research experience for you and the children you work with.

It has been our intention to establish a framework for you to consider and develop your own deep conceptualizations of the many aspects of children, childhood and their roles in the research that they are involved in. We have sought to assist you in understanding how others conceptualize these same aspects and trust that you will give critical considerations to these positions. This book has provided you with a guided walking tour through the research process from the faintest imaginings of a project, through the cut and thrust of planning, organizing and data collection, to the much celebrated revelation of your results to the participants, and the local and the wider research, policy and practice community. From this experience, we anticipate that the tools provided through the provocations of the 'Ponderings', the reflective 'Over to you' activities and the Researcher Capacity Analysis now equip you with a clear framework for doing ethical research with children.

Research with children is courageous work for many reasons. It takes time, sometimes extended periods, in order to authentically document and represent children's views and opinions on matters concerning them. It takes thoughtful and deep consideration about the ethical, moral and political stance you wish to place on children's participation. It takes a great deal of sensitivity, resilience and perseverance in order to be an effective and productive advocate on behalf of children. It also takes the ability to access and influence change agents in policy and practice landscapes in order to act upon children's contributions to our understanding of children and childhood.

So, we encourage you to become a member of a coalition of knowledge generation: building ethical, moral, social and political trust with, about and for children.

Appendix 1

Over to You . . .

The reflection activities presented throughout this book are re-presented here as a planning guide/tool for your use in future research endeavours that will include children.

Phase 1

1 What boundaries or definitions do you place on the following terms?
   a Children
   b Young children
   c Kids
   d Tweens
   e Youth
   f Teenagers
   g Young people
   h Adolescents
2 How do you conceptualize the following 'stages' of childhood?
   a Early years
   b Middle years
   c Adolescence
3 What perspectives do you envisage exist about childhood in non-Euro-Western thinking?
4 How does your definition of child sit with your definition of children? How does this then relate to your definition of contemporary childhood?
5 What are your research questions?
6 How do your research questions relate to how you see children and childhood?

7 Of what benefit is your research project going to be
   a For the children who participate?
   b For children more generally?
8 How would you go about gaining informed consent from a four-year-old child?
9 How will you know if the child fully understands the nature of the research proposed?
10 How will you validate that the consent given by the child is in fact what the child wants?
11 To what extent will your project preparations consider how children and their perspectives are included over the entire research process?
12 What will be the main role/s of the children in your project?
13 What does Article 12.1 of the United Nations Convention on the Rights of the Child (UNCRC) mean to you?
   a How will Article 12.1 impact your study?
   b To what extent do your research questions respond to Article 12.1 of the UNCRC?
14 How does your planned project consider the mandate offered by Article 13 of the UNCRC?
15 Will you have sole responsibility for the children's safety and well-being during the study?
16 How will you ensure the children's behaviour remains safe?
17 Will the children understand which of your instructions are non-negotiable?
   a How will you communicate these instructions?
   b Are there any consequences for non-compliance?

Phase 2

1 What is your theoretical understanding of children and childhood?
2 What roles do you expect the children in your study will have?
3 How will you recruit your participants?
   a Why will you recruit your participants this way?
4 Which gatekeepers do you see as critical in convincing that you have an ethically sound project proposal?
5 Define what the active participation of children in research means to you.
   a What should it look and feel like in practice?
6 Draw your research project timeline.
   a How much time have you allocated to getting to know the children and the research setting?
   b What will be the impact of this timing on your relationship with the children?

7   Using your current role and institution as a researcher, compose a brief introduction of yourself to the children at your local school who are

a   a group of four-year-olds;

b   a group of eight-year-olds;

c   a group of 13-year-olds.

8   Write a potential script for explaining the why, what, when and where of your project to a group of six-year-old children in their second year of primary school.

a   Consider what you know about six-year-olds and the kind of language they might be familiar with.

b   Is your script going to be adequate for all children in the group?

9   What do you need in your 'tool kit' in order to engage with children who speak a language other than yours?

Phase 3

1   What are the key elements in your study that you will need to ensure you keep at the forefront of your ethical practice?

2   A child really wants to be involved in your project but the parents have not given their consent. What should you do?

3   A boy of 11 years of age becomes clearly agitated in a small group conversation group. What can you do to support him?

4   You really want to use drawings as one of the data collection methods because they look good in publications, but the five-year-old boys do not like drawing. How will you proceed?

Phase 4

1   What is your potential five-year dissemination plan for your current study?

a   Conference/s

b   Journal publication/s

c   Book chapter/s

d   Professional magazine/s

e   Grant application/s

f   Teaching/professional material

g   Other

Appendix 2

Researcher Capacity Analysis: individual

Researcher attributes		
Team member name:		
Attribute/s		Available/ required?
Skills		
Qualifications		
Experience		
Roles		
Training		

Researcher Capacity Analysis: project

Project attributes			
Project title:			
Attribute/s		Available/ required?	Team member
Skills			
Qualifications			
Experience			
Roles			
Training			

Appendix 3

Sample information letter to parents

INFORMATION LETTER TO PARENTS

TITLE OF PROJECT: Children's rights education: Rhetoric or action on early childhood practice?

PRINCIPAL INVESTIGATOR: Professor XX

CO-INVESTIGATOR: Professor XX

Dear Parents,

We are seeking permission to invite your child to participate in a study we are undertaking that documents young children's viewpoints on their rights as children within their prior-to-school/school experiences. The project proposal has won the 2010 Jean Denton Memorial Scholarship, and as such has been reviewed by a panel of respected early childhood experts. This early learning centre has agreed to participate.

By undertaking this study, we hope to include young children's voices in wider conversations on children's rights so that teachers and parents, policy-makers and the early childhood community more generally, will carefully consider children's rights from multiple viewpoints. Alongside the researchers, and in the role of a co-researcher, children will be invited to discuss (in small groups), represent (through conversation, drawing, painting, writing etc.) and engage with (class discussions, making lists, recognizing rights in daily life etc.) the topic of children's rights as does, or may in the future, relate to their experience at the early learning centre. This study should benefit children by addressing issues that children themselves raise as holders of rights and inform staff at the early learning centre to more appropriately address issues around children's rights and children's rights education. It is not expected that any risk, inconvenience or discomfort will ensue as a result of children participating in this project.

We will work alongside your child's classroom teacher in Terms 1 and 2, attending at a frequency that is mutually agreed upon. The research work will not disrupt the children's day-to-day learning. The project will invite children to express their ideas and opinions about their rights, and it is not anticipated that this will cause any distress or discomfort.

In addition, children's participation in the research will be completely voluntary and they do not have to participate in any part, or at any time, if they do not wish. All child participants will be invited to give their informed consent/dissent at the beginning of the project and this will be reconfirmed during each visit. At the child's discretion, they may choose to engage in a conversation, draw a picture, take photographs or write a narrative about their rights within their prior-to-school/school setting.

Please note that while every effort will be made to keep the identity of your child confidential, the children may choose to write their name on their work, or they may choose to take a photograph that identifies other children. Please let us know if you prefer not to have your child's image included in any subsequent presentations or publications. The name of the school, classroom, class teacher and your child's surname will not be used in any material that ensues from the project, including any university or professional presentations, or publications. All information will be safely stored at the university. At all times the right of privacy, confidentially and respect for the child will be observed.

Your relationship with your school will not be affected should you or your child choose not to participate or decide to withdraw from the project.

Any questions regarding this project should be directed to the principal Investigator:

Contact details

This study has been approved by the Human Research Ethics Committee at XXX University. In the event that you have any complaint or concern, or if you have any query that the Investigators have not been able to satisfy, you may write to the Chair of the Human Research Ethics Committee at the Research Services Office:

Chair, HREC contact details

Any complaint or concern will be treated in confidence and fully investigated. The parent/s will be informed of the outcome.

If you agree to participate in this project, you should sign both copies of the Consent Form, retain one copy for your records and return the other copy to the principal Investigator. Results of the research project will be made available to participating families through a Parent Evening.

Professor X   Professor Y

Appendix 4

Sample letter of informed consent for parents

PARENT/GUARDIAN CONSENT FORM

Copy for Parent/Guardian to keep

TITLE OF PROJECT: Children's rights education: rhetoric or action on early childhood practice?

PRINCIPAL INVESTIGATOR: Professor X

CO-INVESTIGATOR: Professor Y

I .... (the parent/guardian) have read and understood the information provided in the Letter to Parents. Any questions I have asked have been answered to my satisfaction. I agree/do not agree (please delete where appropriate) for my child .... to participate in this study in Terms 1 and 2 2011, realizing that I can withdraw my consent at any time without affecting my relationship with the school. I agree that research data collected for the study may be published or may be provided to other researchers in a form that may identify my child through use of their first name.

I agree/do not agree that research data collected for the study may be published or may be provided to other researchers in a form that may identify my child through use of their photograph.

NAME OF PARENT/GUARDIAN: ....

SIGNATURE: ....   DATE: ....

SIGNATURE OF PRINCIPAL INVESTIGATOR:

DATE:...................................

SIGNATURE OF CO INVESTIGATOR:

DATE:...................................

References

Archard, D. (2004) *Children: Rights and Childhood*. London: Routledge.

Aries, P. (1962) *Centuries of Childhood*. Harmondsworth: Penguin Education.

Ary, D., L.C. Jacobs, A. Razavieh and C. Sorensen (2002) *Introduction to Research in Education*. Belmont, CA: Wadsworth/Thomson Learning.

Australian Government (2007) *National Statement on Ethical Conduct in Human Research*. Canberra: National Health and Medical Research Council, The Australian Research Council, Australian Vice Chancellors' Committee.

Australian Government (2011) *Australian Code for the Responsible Conduct of Research – Summary*. Available from www.nhmrc.gov.au/research/research-integrity/summary-australian-code-responsible-conduct-research.

Bessant, J. (2006) The fixed age rule: young people, consent and research ethics. *Youth Studies Australia*, 25(4): 50–7.

Blacker, D. (1993) Education as the normative dimension of philosophical hermeneutics. Paper presented at the annual meeting of the Philosophy of Education Society, New Orleans, LA, March. Available online at www.ed.uiuc.edu/eps/pes-yearbook/93_docs/BLACKER.HTM.

Burns, R.B. (2000) *Introduction to Research Methods*. Frenchs Forest, NSW: Pearson Education.

Clark, A. (2005a) Listening to and involving young children: a review of research and practice, *Early Child Development and Care*, 175(6): 489–506.

Clark, A. (2005b) Talking and listening to young children, in M. Dudek (ed.) *Children's Spaces*, pp. 1–13. London: Architectural Press.

Clark, A. (2010) Young children as protagonists and the role of participatory, visual methods in engaging multiple perspectives, *American Journal of Community Psychology*, 46(1): 115–23.

Clark, A. and P. Moss (2001) *Listening to Young Children: The Mosaic Approach*. London: National Children's Bureau for the Joseph Rowntree Foundation.

Cohen, L., L. Manion and K. Morrison (2007) *Research Methods in Education*. London and New York: Routledge.

Conroy, H. and D. Harcourt (2009) Informed agreement to participate: beginning the partnership with children in research, *Early Child Development and Care*, 179(2): 157–65.

Cook-Sather, A. (2002) Authorizing students' perspectives, *Educational Researcher*, 31(4): 3–14.

Corsaro, W.A. (1997) *The Sociology of Childhood*. Thousand Oaks, CA: Pine Forge Press.

Cruddas, L. (2006) Engaged voices – dialogic interaction and the construction of shared social meanings. Paper presented at the *ESRC Seminar Series Conference* 'Pupil Voice and Participation: Pleasures, Promises and Pitfalls', Nottingham, 22–23 May.

Danby, S. and C. Baker (1998) 'What's the problem?' Restoring social order in the preschool classroom, in I. Hutchby and J. Moran-Ellis (eds), *Children and Social Competence: Arenas of Action*, pp. 157–86. London: Falmer Press.

Denzin, N.K. and Y.S. Lincoln (2000) *Handbook of Qualitative Research*. Thousand Oaks, CA: Sage Publications.

Dockett, S. and B. Perry (2003) Children's views and children's voices in starting school, *Australian Journal of Early Childhood*, 28(1): 12–17.

Dowling, M. (2004) Hermeneutics: an exploration, *Nurse Researcher*, 11(4): 30–9.

Doyle, W. (1986) Classroom organisation and management, in M.C. Wittrock (ed.) *Handbook of Research on Teaching*, pp. 392–427. New York: Macmillan.

Fattore, T., J. Mason and E. Watson (2007) Children's conceptualisation(s) of their well-being, *Social Indicators Research*, 80(1): 5–29.

Fisher, C.B. (2005) Deception Research Involving Children: Ethical Practices and Paradoxes. *Ethics & Behavior*, 15(3): 271–87.

Furedi, F. (2001) *Paranoid Parenting: Abandon your Anxieties and be a Good Parent*. London and New York: Penguin.

Gadamer, H.G. (1976) *Philosophical Hermeneutics*. Berkeley, CA: University of California Press.

Gidley, J. and S. Inayatullah (2002) *Youth Futures: Comparative Research and Transformative Visions*. Westport, CO: Praeger.

Grover, S. (2004) Why won't they listen to us? On giving power and voice to children participating in social research, *Childhood*, 11(1): 81–93.

Harcourt, D. (2011) An encounter with children: seeking meaning and understanding about childhood, *European Early Childhood Education Research Journal*, 19(3): 331–43.

Harcourt, D. and H. Conroy (2005) Informed assent, *Early Child Development and Care*, 175(6): 567–77.

Harcourt, D. and H. Conroy (2011) Informed consent: processes and procedures seeking research partnerships with young children, in D. Harcourt, B. Perry and T. Waller (eds) *Researching Young Children's Perspectives: Debating the Ethics and Dilemmas of Educational Research with Children*. London and New York: Routledge.

Harcourt, D. and J. Sargeant (2011) The challenges of conducting ethical research with children, *Education Inquiry*, 2(3): 421–36.

Hopkins, D. (2002) *A Teacher's Guide to Classroom Research*. Maidenhead: Open University Press.

Jamrozik, A. and T. Sweeney (1996) *Children and Society: The Family, the State and Social Parenthood*. Melbourne, VIC: Macmillan Education.

Jans, M. (2004) Children as citizens: towards a contemporary notion of child participation, *Childhood*, 11(1): 27–44.

Karasavidou, E. (2004) The phobic relation between child and internet: social and psychological parameters. Paper presented at the conference, 'Exploring Cultural Perspectives', Florence, Italy, ICRN Press, 12–17 July.

Kemmis, S. (1988) Action research, in J.P. Keeves (ed.) *Educational Research, Methodology, and Measurement: An International Handbook*. Oxford: Pergamon Press.

King, M. (2007) The sociology of childhood as scientific communication: observations from a social systems perspective, *Childhood*, 14: 193.

Kulynych, J. (2001) No playing in the public sphere: democratic theory and the exclusion of children, *Social Theory and Practice [H.W. Wilson – SSA]*, 27(2): 231–64.

Langeveld, M.J. (2003) *How does the Child Experience the World of Things*, 2(3): 215–23.

Levin, D.E. (1998) *Remote Control Childhood?: Combating the Hazards of Media Culture*. Washington, DC: National Association for the Education of Young Children.

Limber, S. and S. Flekkoy (1995) The UN convention on the rights of the child: its relevance for social scientists, *Social Policy Report*, Ann Arbor, Michigan, Society for Research in Child Development, 9.

Lundy, L. (2007) 'Voice' is not enough: conceptualising Article 12 of the United Nations Convention on the Rights of the Child, *British Educational Research Journal*, 33(6): 927–42.

Mahon, A., C. Glendinning, K. Clarke and G. Craig (1996) Researching children: methods and ethics, *Children and Society*, 10(2): 145–54.

Mason, J. and T. Fattore (eds) (2005) *Children Taken Seriously: In Theory, Policy and Practice*. London: Jessica Kingsley Publishers.

Mayall, B. (2002) *Towards a Sociology for Childhood: Thinking from Children's Lives*. London: Open University Press.

Minichiello, V. (1999) *Handbook for Research Methods in Health Sciences*. Frenchs Forest, NSW: Addison-Wesley/Pearson Education Australia.

Moore, T., M. McArthur and D. Noble-Carr (2008) Little voices and big ideas: lessons learned from children about research, *International Journal of Qualitative Methods*, 7(2): 77–91.

Morss, J.R. (1990) *The Biologising of Childhood: Developmental Psychology and the Darwinian Myth*. Hove, UK and Hillsdale, NJ: Lawrence Erlbaum, Associates.

Muller, P. (1969) *The Tasks of Childhood*. London: Weidenfeld & Nicolson.

Neale, B. (ed.) (2004) *Young Children's Citizenship*. York: Joseph Rowntree Foundation.

Neuman, W.L. (2003) *Social Research Methods: Qualitative and Quantitative Approaches*. Boston, MA: Allyn & Bacon.

Packer, M.J. and R.B. Addison (1989) *Entering the Circle: Hermeneutic Investigation in Psychology*. Albany: State University of New York Press.

Parsons, E.C. (2003) A teacher's use of the environment to facilitate the social development of children, *Journal of Research in Childhood Education*, 18(1): 57–70.

Prasad, A. (2002) The contest over meaning: hermeneutics as an interpretive methodology for understanding texts, *Organizational Research Methods*, 5(1): 12–33.

Prasad, A. (2007) The little emperors of a ubiquitous kingdom: marketing and its impact on vulnerable groups – tweens. Paper presented at the International Market Conference on Marketing & Society, Kozhikode, India, January.

Prout, A. (2005) *The Future of Childhood*. London: RoutledgeFalmer.

Rinaldi, C. (2006) *In Dialogue with Reggio Emilia*. London: Routledge.

Saraga, E. (1998) Children's needs who decides? In M. Langan (ed.) *Welfare: Needs Rights and Risks*. London: Routledge.

Sargeant, J. (2005) Young children's perspectives of their place in the world: the value of an importance filter, Ph.D., University of New England.

Sargeant, J. (2007) Children being children: the value of an 'importance filter', *Journal of Student Wellbeing*, 1(1): 15–30.

Sargeant, J. (2010) The altruism of pre-adolescent children's perspectives on 'worry' and 'happiness' in Australia and England, *Childhood: A Global Journal of Child Research*, 17(3): 411–25.

Sawyer, M.G., F.M. Arney and F.M. Baghurst *et al.* (2001) The mental health of young people in Australia: key findings from the child and adolescent component of the national survey of mental health and well-being, *Australian and New Zealand Journal of Psychiatry*, 35(6): 806–14.

Simpson, B. (2004) *Children and Television*. New York and London: Continuum.

Smith, R., M. Monaghan and B. Broad (2002) Involving young people as co-researchers: facing up to the methodological issues, *Qualitative Social Work*, 1(2): 191–207.

Smith, S.L. and B.J. Wilson (2002) Children's comprehension of and fear reactions to television news, *Media Psychology*, 4(1): 1–26.

Stringer, E.T. (1996) *Action Research: A Handbook for Practitioners*. Thousand Oaks, CA: Sage Publications.

Thomas, N. and J. Campling (2000) *Children, Family, and the State: Decision-making and Child Participation*. Basingstoke and New York: St. Martin's Press.

Thomson, F. (2007) Are methodologies for children keeping them in their place? *Children's Geographies*, 5(3): 207–18.

UNICEF (2004) *State of the World's Children*. UNICEF: Geneva.

United Nations (1989) *Convention on the Rights of the Child*. Geneva: UN.

Valentine, G. (1999) Being seen and heard? The ethical complexities of working with children and young people at home and at school, *Ethics, Place & Environment*, 2(2): 141.

Woodrow, C. (2001) Ethics in early childhood: continuing the conversations, *Australian Journal of Early Childhood*, 26(4): 26–30.

Wright, S. (2001) Drawing and storytelling as a means for understanding children's concepts of the future: research in progress, *Journal of Futures Studies*, 6(2): 1–20.

Index

Locators shown in *italics* refer to tables, figures and examples.

action research
  salience and ethical implications as
    approach, 48
adults, stakeholder
  need and process of ethical clearance
    involving, 54–5
  need to inform about confidentiality
    maintenance, 57
age
  as consideration in child participant
    research, 16–17
  case study of importance in research
    design, *17–18*
Alison (case study)
  community elder and council support, *61*
analysis, data
  lack of child ability to correct, 88
  strengths of including children in, 86–7,
    86, 87
  see also outcomes e.g. dissemination,
    research
analysis, research capacity (RCA)
  case study of RCA use, *37*
  characteristics and role in research
    process, 36–7
  use in action as audit tool, 40–42, *41*
  see also elements e.g. experience, researcher;
    qualifications, researcher; roles,
    researcher; skills, researcher; training,
    researcher

Andrew (case study)
  balancing researcher-participant powers,
    34
  Research Capacity Analysis use, *37*
Anne (case study)
  disrespectful conference presentation,
    94
anonymity, participant
  case study of, *56*
  need and process of ensuring child, 55–7
artefacts
  design considerations for use with
    children, 50–51
audit
  example of RCA as tool for, 40–42, *41*
Australian National Statement on Ethical
    Conduct in Research, 10
authorization, institutional
  role in ensuring ethical research, 59–60

behaviour and mood, child
  challenges of in child participant research,
    18–19
Bessant, J., 28, 36
Blacker, D., 8
Burns, R., 50, 51

cameras
  design considerations for use with
    children, 51

capacities, child
  salience for successful research power
    balance, 33–5, *34*
care, duty of
  UNCRC views on child right to 28
  see also privacy; protection, child
Carmel (case study)
  Research Capacity Analysis use, *37*
case studies and examples
  adherence to ethical codes, *85*
  age and context in research design, *17–18*
  balancing researcher-participant powers,
    34
  challenges of research method and tool
    selection, *49*
  children's experience of documenting
    consent, *74*
  community elder and council support,
    61
  dilemma of lack of child informed consent,
    73
  dilemmas with participant reporting, *93*
  disrespectful conference presentation, *94*
  ethical and informed child research
    inclusion, *30*
  gaining trust and familiarity of
    participants, *68*
  importance of research question design,
    12
  inclusion of all children in research, *78*
  involving children in data analysis, *86*
  need to consult children about research,
    20, 22
  opening research conversations with
    children, *80*
  parameters of ethical research, *11*
  participant anonymity and confidentiality,
    56
  Research Capacity Analysis use, *37*
  researcher engagement with children, *70*
  role and work of ethics committees, *59*
  role of explanatory statements, *62, 102–3*
  salience and ethical implications of, *48–9*
Charlotte (case study)
  need for ethical and informed child
    research inclusion, *30*
checklists *see* forms and checklists
children and childhood
  case study of lack of child informed
    consent, *73*

case study of researcher engagement with,
    70
  conceptualization of contemporary
    Euro-Western, 4–6
  conceptualizing definitions of, 2–4
  inviting of as research participants, 66–9,
    68
  need to include marginalized in research
    process, 77–9, *78*
  researcher positions on researching with,
    6–10
  role and need for in research, 1–2, 44–5,
    69–70
  see also factors impacting e.g. anonymity,
    participant; confidentiality, participant;
    design, research; ethics; powers,
    researcher-participants; privacy;
    relationships, researcher-participant;
    'sensitive' subjects; tools, data collection;
    UN Convention on the Rights of the
    Child
  see also processes involving e.g. analysis,
    data; consent, informed; conversations,
    research; documentation, consent
Clark, A., 51, 66
clearance, ethical
  need and process of stakeholder and
    participant, 54–5
codes, ethical conduct
  examples of use and purpose, 83–6, *85*
cognition, child
  salience for successful research power
    balance, 33–4, *34*
Cohen, L., 47, 49
collaboration, research
  across languages and cultures, 79
collection, data
  tool design implications for use with
    children, 49–53, *49*
committees, ethics
  case studies of, *59, 61*
  role and processes in research acceptance,
    57–61
  see also councils, governing
communication, modes of
  UNCRC views on child right to, 26–7
  see also 'voice'
conceptualization, research
  purpose of including child perspectives,
    20–23, *20, 22*

conduct, ethical
  examples of use and purpose of codes of,
    83–6, *85*
conferences
  case study of disrespectful presentation at,
    94
  ethics of research dissemination at, 93–4
confidentiality, participant
  case study of, *56*
  need and process of ensuring child, 55–7
consent, informed
  case study and need to enable child
    inclusion, 28–30, *30*
  case study of lack of, *73*
  contents and uses of documents of, 63–4
  documenting of, 74–6, *74, 75, 76*
  elements of process of gaining, 70–73
  sample letter of, 104
  withdrawal of, 77
consent, parental
  need and process of ethical clearance
    involving, 55
consultation, research
  case studies of need for, *20, 22*
  purpose of including child perspectives,
    20–23
  see also conversations, research
context, socio-community
  case study of importance in research
    design, *17–18*
  role as concern in child participant
    research, 17–18
conversations, research
  design considerations for use with
    children, 51–2
  salience of child respondent opening of,
    79–80, *80*
  see also consultation, research
Cook-Sather, A., 3
correction, research
  implications of lack of child ability to,
    88
councils, governing
  case study of importance, *61*
  role in ensuring ethically sound research,
    60
  see also committees, ethics
cultures
  as concern in research with child
    participants, 17–18, *17–18*

research collaboration across languages
    and, 79
data, analysis of
  lack of child ability to correct, 88
  strengths of including children in, 86–7,
    86, 87
data, collection of
  tool design implications for use with
    children, 49–53, *49*
Deborah (case study and example)
  children's experience of documenting
    consent, *74*
  informed consent form used by, 63, 104
  of involving children in data analysis, *86*
  opening research conversations with
    children, *80*
  role of explanatory statements, *62,
    102–3*
demographics
  as consideration in research with child
    participants, 15–16
descriptive research
  salience and ethical implications as
    approach, 47–8
design, research
  characteristics and importance of
    UNCRC, 23–8
  considerations in relation to sensitive
    subjects, 53
  considerations when involving children,
    14–19, *15, 17–18*
  implications of data collection tools,
    49–53, *49*
  purpose of child consultation and
    perspectives, 19–23, *20, 22*
  see also collaboration, research
  see also elements e.g. anonymity, participant;
    confidentiality, participant; consent,
    informed; ethics; inclusion, research;
    questions, research; recruitment,
    researcher
devices, recording
  design considerations for use with
    children, 51
disability
  as concern in research with child
    participants, 17–18, *17–18*
dissemination, research
  case study of dilemmas with participant
    reporting, *93*

ethics and case study of conference and
  seminar, 93–4, *94*
reporting back to participants as element
  of, 92–3
documentation, consent
  children's experience of, 74–6, *74*, *75*, *76*
Doyle, W., 9

Edward (case study)
  need to adhere to ethical conduct codes,
  85
elders, community
  case study of importance, *61*
  role in ensuring ethically sound research,
  60
Emma (case study)
  role and work of ethics committees, *59*
emotions, child
  salience for successful research power
  balance, 33
ethics
  case study, definition and implications for
  research, 10–12, *11*
  case study and need for to enable child
  inclusion, 28–30, *30*
  importance of research design for,
  45–9
  need and process of ethical clearance,
  54–5
  role, processes and case studies of
  committees of, 57–61, *59*, *61*
  see also codes, ethical conduct
  see also arenas for application e.g.
  dissemination, research
ethnography
  salience and ethical implications as
  research approach, 46–7
Europe
  conceptualization of children and
  childhood in, 4–6
examples *see* case studies and examples
experience, researcher
  importance and role as element of RCA,
  38–9
experiences, child life
  consideration of impact on as element of
  research design, 15
experimentation
  characteristics as approach to research
  with children, 9–10

explanation
  salience as element of informed consent,
  70–72

'face value'
  characteristics as approach to research
  with children, 8–9
familiarity, feelings of
  case study and salience of gaining
  respondent, 67–9, *68*
Fisher, C., 28
Flekkoy, S., 24, 29
focus groups
  design considerations for use with
  children, 51
forms and checklists
  contents and uses of consent, 63–4
  example of informed consent, 104
  RCA checklist for individuals, 100
  RCA checklist for projects, 101

gatekeepers
  importance at research design stage, 53–4
gender
  as concern in research with child
  participants, 17–18, *17–18*
Gérard (case study)
  parameters of ethical research, *11*
governance, councils of
  case study of importance, *61*
  role in ensuring ethically sound research, 60
  see also committees, ethics
groups, focus
  design considerations for use with
  children, 51
Grover, S., 3, 20, 31

'Hawthorne Effect', 48
hermeneutics
  characteristics as approach to research
  with children, 8–9
Human Research Ethics Committees
  (HRECs), 54

inclusion, research
  need for ethical and informed child
  inclusion, 28–30, *30*
institutions, stakeholder
  need and process of ethical clearance
  involving, 54–5

need for confidentiality and anonymity
maintenance, 57
role in ensuring ethical research
authorisation, 59–60
interest, loss of
challenge of with research involving
children, 18
interviews
design considerations for use with
children, 51
introductions, researcher-participant
need and importance, 69–70
invitations, research
importance of extending, 73–4

Jack (case study)
dilemma of lack of informed consent,
73
James (case study)
challenges of research method and tool
selection, *49*
Jeremy (case study)
inclusion of all children in research, *78*
Jonathan (case study and example)
of involving children in data analysis, *87*
participant anonymity and confidentiality,
56

Kelvin (case study)
researcher engagement with children,
70
King, M., 7
Kulynych, J., 29

languages
as concern in research with child
participants, 17–18, *17–18*
research collaboration across cultures and,
79
letters
example of information, 102–3
example of informed consent, 104
letters, information
role in ensuring ethically sound research,
61–2, *62*
sample explanatory statement, 102–3
lifestyles, child
consideration of impact on as element of
research design, 15
Limber, S., 24, 29

marginalization
as concern in research with child
participants, 17–18, *17–18*
Mayall, B., 1, 29
methods, research *see* tools, data collection
Minichiello, V., 51
mood and behaviour, child
challenges of in child participant research,
18–19
Moss, P., 51

Neale, B., 29
Neuman, W., 52

observation, participant
salience and ethical implications as
research approach, 47
Ole (case study)
importance of age and context in research
design, *17–18*

parents
need for consent and clearance from,
54–5
role in ensuring ethically sound research,
61
sample information letter to, 102–3
sample letter of informed consent for,
104
Parsons, E., 9
participants, research
case study and salience of feelings of trust
in gaining, 67–9, *68*
need and process of ensuring anonymity
and confidentiality of, 55–7, *56*
need and process of ethical clearance
involving, 54–5
reporting back to as element of
dissemination, 92–3
see also introductions, researcher-
participant; powers, researcher-
participant; relationships,
researcher-participant
see also particular e.g. children
peers, reviews by
role in ensuring ethical research,
59–60
phenomenology
salience and ethical implications as
research approach, 46

Philip (case study)
  need to consult children at start of
      research, *20*
Phoebe (case study)
  importance of research question design, *12*
populations
  as consideration in research with child
      participants, 15–16
positivism
  characteristics as approach to research
      with children, 9–10
powers, researcher-participant
  case study of balancing, *34*
  salience of balancing of for successful
      research, 31–5
presentations, conference
  case study of disrespectful, *94*
privacy
  importance of discussing with child
      respondents, 80–81
  UNCRC views on child right to, 27
  see also care, duty of; protection, child
projects, research *see* research
protection, child
  UNCRC views on child right to, 27–8
  see also care, duty of; privacy
psychology, child
  salience for successful research power
      balance, 34–5

qualifications, researcher
  importance and role as element of RCA,
      38
qualitative and quantitative research
  salience and ethical implications as
      approach, 46
questions, research
  case study, role and importance in
      research design, 12–13, *12*
  design considerations for use with
      children, 52–3

Rachel (case study)
  Research Capacity Analysis use, *37*
RCA *see* Research Capacity Analysis
recording, devices of
  design considerations for use with
      children, 51
recruitment, researcher
  considerations at design stage, 53–4

reflexivity, personal
  topic list for phase four processes, 95–6,
      99
  topic list for phase one processes, 42–3,
      97–8
  topic list for phase three processes, 89–90,
      99
  topic list for phase two processes, 64–5,
      98–9
relationships, researcher-participant
  salience and need for effective, 30–31
  see also elements e.g. powers,
      researcher-participant
religion
  as concern in research with child
      participants, 17–18, *17–18*
Renee (case study)
  need to consult children about research,
      22
reports, research
  importance as element of research
      dissemination, 92
research
  case study, definition and features of
      ethical, 10–12, *11*
  collaboration across languages and
      cultures, 79
  role and need for children within, 1–2,
      44–5
  see also elements and methods e.g. analysis,
      correction, research; data; design,
      research; dissemination, research; ethics;
      reflexivity, personal; tools, data
      collection
  see also players e.g. adults; children; parents
  see also types e.g. descriptive research;
      ethnography; phenomenology;
      qualitative and quantitative research;
      'sensitive' research
Research Capacity Analysis (RCA)
  case study of RCA uses, *37*
  characteristics and role in research
      process, 36–7
  checklists for individuals and projects, 100,
      101
  use in action as audit tool, 40–42, *41*
  see also elements e.g. experience, researcher;
      qualifications, researcher; roles,
      researcher; skills, researcher; training,
      researcher

researchers
  position on researching with children,
    6–10
  RCA audit template assessing individual,
    41
  RCA checklist for individual, 100
  see also experience, researcher;
    qualifications, researcher; roles,
    researcher; skills, researcher; training,
    researcher
  see also specific factors involving e.g. powers,
    researcher-participant, relationships,
    researcher-participant
researchers-teachers
  delicacy of balance of for successful
    relationships, 31–2
respondents, research see participants,
    research
reviews, peer
  role in ensuring ethical research, 59–60
roles, researcher
  importance and role as element of RCA,
    39

Sarah (case study)
  dilemmas with participant reporting, 93
schools, stakeholder
  need and process of ethical clearance
    involving, 54–5
security, feelings of
  case study of gaining respondent, 68
  salience as feature of gaining participants,
    67–9
seminars
  case study of disrespectful presentation at,
    94
  ethics of research dissemination at,
    93–4
'sensitive' subjects
  considerations when using children in
    research, 53
size, physical
  salience of child for successful research
    power balance, 33
skills, researcher
  importance and role as element of RCA,
    37–8
skills, social
  salience of child for successful research
    power balance, 35

stakeholders
  need and process of ethical clearance
    involving, 54–5
  need to inform about confidentiality
    maintenance, 57
  role of institutional in ensuring research
    authorisation, 59–60
statements, explanatory
  role in ensuring ethically sound research,
    61–2, 62
  sample explanatory statement,
    102–3
status, socio-economic
  as concern in research with child
    participants, 17–18, 17–18
stranger-researcher
  delicacy of balance of for successful
    relationships, 32
studies (case studies) see case studies
studies, pilot
  uses in data collection tool testing, 49
subjects, sensitive
  considerations when using children in
    research, 53
Sue (case study)
  gaining of participant trust and familiarity,
    68
surveys
  design considerations for use with
    children, 50

teachers-researchers
  delicacy of balance of for successful
    relationships, 31–2
templates
  Research Capacity Analysis audit, 41
Thomson, F., 2
tools, audit
  example of RCA as, 40–42, 41
tools, data collection
  design implications for use with children,
    49–53, 49
training, researcher
  importance and role as element of RCA,
    39–40
trust, feelings of
  case study of gaining respondent
    familiarity and, 68
  salience as feature of gaining participants,
    67–9

UN Convention on the Rights of the Child
(UNCRC)
characteristics and importance, 23–8
recommendations concerning child
communication, 70

viewpoints
importance of including child in research,
1–2
of researchers on researching children, 7–8

'voice'
UNCRC views on child right to, 24–6
see also communication, mode of

world, western
conceptualization of children and
childhood in, 4–6
Wright, S., 50

DOING EARLY CHILDHOOD RESEARCH

Glenda Mac Naughton

9780335242627 (Paperback)
July 2010

"It is rare for any research methodology book to cover so much ground, and contain so many different kinds of resources between two covers."
Journal of Education for Teaching

The book provides a thorough introduction to the most common research methods used in the early childhood context. The book covers a wide range of conventional and newer methods including:

- Observation
- Surveys and interviews with adults and children
- Action research
- Ethnography
- Quasi-experimental approaches

Doing Early Childhood Research explains clearly how to set up research projects which are theoretically grounded, well-designed, rigorously analysed, feasible and ethically based. Each chapter is illustrated with examples.

www.openup.co.uk

PARENTS AND PROFESSIONALS
IN EARLY CHILDHOOD SETTINGS

Glenda MacNaughton and Patrick Hughes

9780335243730 (Paperback)
2011

eBook also available

Parents and Professionals in Early Childhood Settings addresses the
complex and sometimes controversial issues that emerge from the care
and education of young children. Staff and parents in early childhood
settings can find ample advice about how to promote good communication,
but much of that advice has no grounding in their daily lives. Instead, it
prescribes an established set menu of communication tools, such as
newsletters, notebooks and message boards that rarely respond to what
staff and families say about relationships between them.

Key features:

- Covers a range of 'issue stories' which the reader can dip into as
  appropriate and which draw on research into relationships between
  staff and families
- Each chapter or story will feature the voices and perspectives of 'real
  staff' and families, illustrating the complex, difficult and/or
  controversial issue and highlighting the questions of power and
  knowledge that emerge
- Fairness Alerts to help the reader see, understand and break unfair
  thinking habits

www.openup.co.uk

 OPEN UNIVERSITY PRESS
McGraw - Hill Education

**INTERPROFESSIONAL
WORKING IN PRACTICE**
Learning and Working Together
for Children and Families

Lyn Trodd and Leo Chivers

9780335244478 (Paperback)
2011

eBook also available

The authors draw on their experiences of a wide range of professional
heritages and contexts to propose that a new professionalism is required
in an interprofessional world. The book argues that individuals cannot
learn to work interprofessionally in the complex, ever changing world of
services for children and families, without gaining considerable
understanding of interprofessionalism and internalizing appropriate values
and principles.

The book offers new thinking on the challenges of interprofessional
working including exploration of leading in uncertainty and its underpinning
principles and values.

Key features:

- Chapters grouped into related strands of context, learning, working
  and current and future challenges
- Case studies and practice dilemmas designed to challenge the
  reader
- Reflexivity points

www.openup.co.uk